Be Nice
(Or Else!)
and what's in it for you

People Are Talking About

BE NICE (OR ELSE!)

"*BE NICE (OR ELSE!)* by Winn Claybaugh is one of the most accurate books of today. Being nice—in my personal and business life—has helped me, and I know this book will definitely benefit *anyone* who reads it. Exceptionally well done, Winn!"

— **John Paul DeJoria**

Co-founder and CEO of Paul Mitchell salon hair care products

"I thoroughly enjoyed it. What a brilliant approach to this topic: multilayered and excellent take-home value. As a consumer of this topic, I learned a lot. I think this book is so right on target—and I'm *not* just being nice!"

— **Leeza Gibbons**

TV and Radio Personality

Founder of the Leeza Gibbons Memory Foundation

"One has to admire Winn Claybaugh. He seems to spend his life uplifting our craft and everyone else's as well. He's so positive in his rationale of life that just by reading his book you want to be nice. Of course in the craft of hair, we have an advantage. Our sole purpose is to make another human being look and feel elated about themselves, as they perceive the sense of change—what could be nicer than that?"

— **Vidal Sassoon**

"Full of accessible and down-to-earth advice, *BE NICE (OR ELSE!)* could well be the instruction manual for the growing kindness movement."

— **Catherine Ryan Hyde**

Author of *Pay It Forward, Electric God,* and *Walter's Purple Heart*

President of the Pay It Forward Foundation

"*BE NICE (OR ELSE!)* is the perfect road map to creating a happy life for yourself and those around you. Kindness can inspire others, defuse anger, bring hope, heal pain, and change the world."

— **David Wagner**

    Author of *Life as a Daymaker*

    Founder of JUUT Salonspas

"Winn Claybaugh is a natural-born storyteller whose influence on the people around him has made a difference in their lives. Winn is a testament to his niceness and what it can do."

— **Joan Harrison**

    Editorial Director, *Canadian Hairdresser* magazine

"*BE NICE (OR ELSE!)* is an absolute must for anyone who wants to succeed in business and in life. This insightful manual—interspersed with humor, sage advice, interactive exercises, and plenty of wisdom— demystifies the art of being nice and makes it accessible to everyone. It's chock-a-block with very nice ideas indeed, and ones that the world truly does need more of!"

— **Kelley Donahue**

    Executive Editor, *American Salon* magazine

"Winn Claybaugh's uncommonly warm, witty approach to common-sense principles of success have inspired audiences and readers for years. With *BE NICE (OR ELSE!)*, he has created a genuinely practical handbook for finishing first in life and business. Nice ideas, nice stories, nice touch."

— **Michele Musgrove**

    Editorial Director, Modern Salon Media

Be Nice (Or Else!)

and what's in it for you

By
Winn Claybaugh

Foreword by Larry King

Von Curtis Publishing

Be Nice (Or Else!)
© 2004 by Winn Claybaugh

Von Curtis Publishing
1278 Glenneyre, Ste. 96
Laguna Beach, CA 92651
Tel: (800) 459-4007
Fax: (949) 497-7163
E-mail: info@BeNiceOrElse.com
Web: www.BeNiceOrElse.com

Edited by Gail Fink

Printed in the United States

ATTENTION: ORGANIZATIONS and CORPORATIONS
Bulk quantity discounts for reselling, gifts,
or fundraising are available.
For more information, please contact the Von Curtis Publishing
sales department. Tel: (800) 459-4007

ISBN 0-9749939-9-9
LCCN 2004102708

To my Grandma LaRue, my mother Jeanne,
and my two sisters, Ann and Connie
– *the nicest people I know!*

In grateful and loving memory of my
dear friend, Denis Hand.

CONTENTS

FOREWORD

Winn Claybaugh is a remarkable guy and one of the best motivational speakers in the country. In this terrific work, he brings the reader easy-to-use concepts that could bring interesting rewards.

A famous swami once told me years ago that someone who's nice always gains. He told me that if you wake up in the morning and immediately say that this day was a total gift, that you had no "right" to the day, then it wouldn't matter if it were raining or cloudy or whatever.

If the toast you got is burnt, the best way to get proper toast is to be nice to the waitress. The best way to get your co-workers to like you is to smile when you go to work. The smiler has the upper hand. So, follow carefully Winn's adept advice. Use the book in your daily life and you'll find life just keeps on getting better. You better do this or I'll kill you.

— **Larry King**

INTRODUCTION

As a motivational speaker on the road for many years, I used to beat around the bush in my seminars when it came to the topic of creating a better work environment or a happier home life. I'd preach the same words that had been passed down from generation to generation at every "rah-rah" seminar ever held, sidestepping the issue by encouraging my audience to just "Be positive" or "Have a good attitude."

To tell the truth, the blissful "Kum-ba-ya" philosophy I presented onstage seemed more unattainable to me than I proposed. Why? Because I personally had not yet learned the simple secret to creating happiness at work and at home.

Then one night I was watching the Biography channel, and they showed a story on the Disney theme parks. The program described the training process for Disney employees—training on how to "be nice." The final message of the show was, "Heaven help the Disney employee who is not nice." That was it! How straightforward and trouble-free. The end result I'd longed for was a simpler path than I'd imagined. I could just remove all the dogma and boil the philosophies down to one simple message: Heaven help ANYONE who's not nice. Once I consciously chose to adopt that same philosophy into my personal and business life, all of a sudden my stride was greater and my results more profound.

Do I possess the knowledge or skill to perform brain surgery? No, and it's doubtful that I ever will in this lifetime. But I can master being nice, and I can be effective at it today. Can I win a marathon? Not today, but I can be nice today. Can I run a multimillion-dollar company? Maybe someday, but I can be nice right now . . . and so can you.

Anyone Can Be Nice

In a world where you have to be computer literate, business savvy, a master negotiator, and professionally dressed, you must also be nice. You can be artistically brilliant, but you'd better be nice. You can be a gifted salesperson, a talented musician, or a great athlete, but you'd better be nice. Heaven help the person who isn't nice!

Being nice is so easy, and its rewards are limitless and immeasurable. Let's say you meet or know someone who's shy, depressed, or lonely. What will most easily communicate with that person and give them permission to trust you and open up to you? Your wealth? Your good looks? Your intelligence? Hardly. Try being nice.

Go ahead and work on your knowledge of how to be a more effective salesperson. Go ahead and work on your resume and your college degree. Build your investment portfolio. Climb that corporate ladder. And while you're doing all that, why not develop the most important skill a person could have: being nice.

You can have the most manicured lawn on the block, but add being nice and you'll see neighbors bend over backward to keep an eye on your property while you're vacationing. You might be incredible at what you do for a living, but add being nice to the formula and watch co-workers work extra hard to make your marketing presentation sing.

When you add being nice to what you're good at, your relationships will flourish and your career will skyrocket. If you're a talented doctor and being nice is part of your skill set, your office will always be full. If you're a talented hairdresser and you add being nice to your hairdressing skills, you'll make more money than you ever dreamed possible.

Being nice will open doors, get you what you need, bring you the attention or help you desire, and leave a more immediate and lasting impression than any other character trait, personality gesture, or physical feature you possess. Being nice is a skill that can be marketed and sold.

Before you read any further, let me make one thing perfectly clear. I'm not advocating that you *pretend* to be nice in order to make sales, attract lovers, or manipulate people in any way. To be effective, being nice must be genuine.

A few years ago, I came across an ad in one of those magazines you see on an airplane. It said: NEGTIATING TO GET WHAT YOU WANT. I don't remember the company's name or what they sold, but I'll never forget the philosophy they promoted: Kill or be killed, winner take all, the only way to win is for everyone else to lose. Nowhere in the ad did they even consider the idea of negotiating in a way that benefits the other side. This "for me to win, you have to lose" mentality is far too common in society today. BE NICE is a different approach—when you start being nice, everybody wins.

The Ultimate Compliment: "And He's SO NICE! "

Not long ago, a friend of mine was talking about a new love interest she'd recently met. In describing him, she went into great detail about his physical traits, his career success, and his financial achievements. But the icing on the cake—the one trait she saved for last, even after describing everything else—was, "And he's SO NICE!"

Being called nice is the ultimate compliment. It's worth celebrating when you have the fortune to discover it in others because, unfortunately, encountering a nice person is so rare that it almost comes as a surprise. Beautiful bodies are a dime a dozen. You can walk into any gym and find plenty of in-shape, beautiful people, but how wonderful it is when you discover a stud or a hottie who's also nice. You can walk into any busy restaurant and find lots of cranky waitresses or waiters, but what a pleasure it is to be served by someone nice.

On the other hand, you've probably met people somewhere along the line who impressed you with their wit, their charm, their style, their success, their money, or perhaps their celebrity. Then you got to know them and something heartbreaking happened: You discovered that they weren't nice. Perhaps they had a constant dribble of negativity toward others. Maybe every other word out of their mouths was about how wonderful they were and how awful some other person was. From that point on, any positive trait or talent they had seemed instantly invalidated. When you're not nice, everything else goes right down the drain.

You could attend a party driving the finest car and wearing the perfect clothes—but with a nasty, judgmental attitude—and what lasting impression would you leave? Not nice. But attend the same party, driving the same car and wearing the same clothes—and smile as you introduce yourself to everyone and ask them questions about themselves—and you'll be known as the most available bachelor or bachelorette in town.

Are You Ready?

In the pages that follow, you'll learn what it means to be nice and, even more important, what it means not to be. You'll discover that being nice begins with you: Before you can be nice in the world, you have to be nice to yourself. You might even have to fall in love with yourself. By doing such a radical thing, you'll then be able to expand your "circle of nice" to the rest of the world: your family, friends, co-workers, and strangers. You'll also learn what to do when you blow it (and I promise you, you will blow it from time to time)—how to repair the damage and keep from repeating the same mistakes again and again. Last but certainly not least, you'll discover a host of ways to spread this BE NICE movement to the rest of the world.

In my seminars, I've always tried to avoid saying, "Let me *teach* this to you." Instead, I say, "Let me *share* this with you," because I feel as though I need to learn the information as much as anyone in my audience. With this book, I feel the same way. When it comes to being nice, I blow it a lot. I do the exact opposite of my BE NICE intentions, and I have to remind myself daily of my strong commitment to being nice. However, I can honestly say that my aim, my purpose, and my sincere desire in life is to be nice. I'm my mother's son, and my mother taught me well. I'm earnestly looking for passionate individuals who want to join me in this journey. Let's study the curriculum; work on ourselves; and practice, practice, practice with others. Then together, let's charm others to this simpler way of life.

If you're ready to join me in an exciting new adventure, then to quote a very courageous man on an airplane on September 11, "Let's roll."

◪ ◪ ◪

Nice Guys DO NOT Finish Last!

"I expect to pass through life but once. If, therefore, there be any kindness
I can show, or any good thing I can do to any fellow being,
let me do it now, for I shall not pass this way again."
—**William Penn**

As I was contemplating this book, I talked about it everywhere I went. When I asked people for their thoughts and opinions about the topic of being nice, I received a very consistent reaction: "If I'm nice, people will walk all over me."

Being nice doesn't mean becoming a doormat. It doesn't mean speaking in a soft voice and wearing pastel colors, and it certainly doesn't mean letting people walk all over you.

Contrary to the old saying, nice guys do not finish last. You can have an opinion, and still be nice. You can tell people when they've wronged you, and still be nice. You can disagree with someone, and still be nice about it. You can "be about business" and still be nice.

Nice people get divorced, quit jobs, get fired, struggle with addictions, get traffic tickets, have bad things happen to them, and even have financial problems. Nice people can be found in many types of careers, in hundreds of different religions, in every race and color, and in every country on the planet. Nice people can be old, young, straight, gay, male, female, large, tiny, and everything in between. Unfortunately, so can mean people. So, before you read much further, let's make sure you can tell the difference.

A Person Who Does Nice Things
Is Not Necessarily a Nice Person

Being philanthropic or doing volunteer work is not necessarily the same thing as being nice. You can be nice without volunteering at a nursing home. Conversely, you could volunteer at a nursing home and not be a nice person. Volunteer work may account for a couple of hours per month of your time, but you can be nice twenty-four hours a day. Being nice is a full-time commitment and lifestyle.

A Person Who Acts Like the Center of the Universe
Is Not a Nice Person

A wonderful storyteller by the name of C. W. Metcalf shared a story about a man in the airport who was verbally abusing an airline ticketing agent. It seems that the traveler had missed his flight due to mechanical difficulties. Apparently, the man was very loud, demonstrative, and mean to the poor ticketing agent, who obviously had no control over the plane's condition. C. W. went up to the abusive man and asked, "Can I have your autograph?" When the man, puzzled and confused, asked, "Why do you want my autograph?" C. W. responded, "Because I've never met the center of the universe before!"

Mean people oftentimes do get more attention and better service than people who are patient and nice. Someone who has the "nerve" to be aggressive and demanding somehow seems better equipped to "get the job done" or to "be about business." But when you think about the people who are aggressive, loud, and mean in order to get attention and immediate service, are they really that much further ahead? So they get up to their hotel room ten minutes faster than the hotel guest who was patient. Does that really add value to their lives?

A Person Who's Nice to You but Mean to a Waitress
Is Not a Nice Person

As humor writer Dave Barry wrote in his book *Dave Barry Turns 50,* "A person who is nice to you, but rude to the waiter, is not a nice person." As you consider this "being nice" thing, I'm sure you'd agree that being nice could definitely give a person the upper hand. However, there are some people who know who to be nice to in order to get what they want but forgo the practice in other situations. Being nice is about *inclusiveness,* not *exclusiveness.* You can't pick and choose to whom you are nice.

Have you ever had this experience? You meet someone new who you think is a really nice person. He or she may even display that charm and niceness for months. Then one night the two of you are out to dinner, in the middle of a lovely conversation, when the waitress makes a mistake and your date lets her have it. Suddenly, the nice guy you thought was the Gandhi of "take home to Mom" boyfriends becomes the Freddy Krueger date-from-hell. Or the Mother Teresa "this could be the one" girlfriend changes into a Mommy Dearest nightmare. What used to be beautiful, endearing, and cute about the person suddenly becomes ugly, embarrassing, and *done.*

You see this all the time, don't you? It even comes up on television, where it may be slightly exaggerated but not far from the truth. In an episode of the TV show *Friends,* Rachel was dating a guy she believed to be a really nice person. While on a double date with her friend Ross, Rachel slipped out to the ladies room with Ross's date, and Ross witnessed Rachel's date screaming and belittling two people for sitting in the wrong theater seats. The rest of the episode had Ross trying to entrap Rachel's new boyfriend into losing his cool and displaying that mean, nasty side of him.

What Keeps People from Being Nice?

Actions create habits, and habits form your character and personality. Bad habits lead to bad luck. Good habits lead to good luck. Nice guys cultivate good habits, which lead to good luck and a good life. If you want a good life, create good habits and avoid bad habits like the ones that follow.

◙ Being a Whiner

Do you know people who seem as though they were programmed for misery, and they want to make sure you're miserable, too? They show up to work, pull you aside, and say, "You think your life is bad? Wait till you hear what happened to me!" They can't wait to tell you about their drama. Being a whiner is a very bad habit, and it's one of the traits of a not-nice person.

▣ Being Exclusive

As you unfold this BE NICE lifestyle, you'll meet individuals who treat some people nicely to get what they want, while excluding everyone else from their circle of nice. That's not what this book is about. If your mindset is that some people are excluded from your niceness simply because they can't do anything for you, then you've missed the mark.

▣ Being Afraid Your Needs Won't Be Met

Some people have a stronger belief in "scarcity" than in "abundance." They believe there's only so much to go around, so they must grab their share before other people do or they might miss out. They want to grab their share of happiness, money, opportunity, and anything else they believe is in short supply. That grabbing gets in the way of being nice.

▣ Being Late

One of the things I hear most often when I ask about the habits of not-nice people is, "It's not nice to be late and keep someone waiting." When you're late, you give people the perception (whether it's true or not) that your time, your objectives, and your agenda are more important than anyone else's. In a later chapter, you'll discover the difference between perception and reality, but if people have a perception that you're not a nice person (even though the reality may be different), you still have to own and deal with that perception.

▣ Having Bad Manners

Being the bearer of a Platinum Visa card is not a license to be mean or rude. I know what it feels like to plop down one of those cards and then look around to make sure enough people saw it. It gives you an air of confidence, an attitude of superiority. It's the same as when you sit in the first-class section on an airplane. Those wide leather seats seem to divide "you" from "them." In your mind, they divide royalty from peasants, a filet mignon meal from a peanut snack.

A good friend of mine is a flight attendant for one of the major airline corporations. She tells story after story about airline passengers who act as though they're the only people aboard. They seem to believe that every flight attendant is there to serve only them. Such passengers will flash their Gold Medallion cards as though they were then excused and exempt from practicing any niceties or manners, as if that card gave them the right to be impolite and rude.

Bad manners run rampant in our society, and it's one of the most common habits that keep people from being nice.

Character Traits and Actions That Are Not Nice

You could be a naturally nice person, but if you do any of the following, you'll diminish your nice factor.

▣ Being a Policing Agent

This is one of those symptoms I continuously have to watch for in myself: always inspecting and policing other people's behaviors, moods, actions, and attitudes. I want to police the way total strangers drive on the freeway. I want to police the way the man across the restaurant chews his food. I want to police the clothes you wear, how you speak to your kids, how you slump in your chair, how you . . . *and I don't even know you!*

But it gets worse. If I *do* know you, then of *course* I need to monitor your every move, word, sound, thought, action—and, oh yeah, how you spend your money. I realize you didn't ask for my advice, but you're going to get it anyway. After all, I care about you, and I don't want you to get hurt by wearing your hair the wrong way or dating the wrong person.

▣ Being a Critic

My brother Brennan happens to work for me in my company. Until recently, Brennan strongly disliked sushi and had no problem letting everyone know. Whenever dinner decisions were being made with a group of friends, and sushi was suggested, he would immediately and strongly express his distaste. Brennan is always looking for ways to advance in his career, and it finally occurred to me (which I promptly shared with Brennan) that many of my business dealings and negotiations are held in sushi restaurants. I said to him, "Imagine that a person with a great offer or opportunity for you suggested, 'Let's meet and discuss this over sushi.' What do you think would happen if you responded, '*Eeewww!* I hate sushi'?" My recommendation to Brennan was that he stop critiquing sushi and learn to find something on the menu to order and enjoy. Brennan now enjoys all of his dining experiences, and some of them happen to take place in sushi restaurants.

▣

In my company, we strongly believe in the importance of lifelong learning, and we heavily invest in training our people. Years ago, I'd spend a lot of money purchasing airline tickets, hotel rooms, and seminar tuition to send my people to educational events in fun places like Las Vegas. When they'd return, I'd always ask, "So how was it?" On occasion, they'd respond with, "I didn't like the food they served at lunch." I'd think to myself, *Who cares what you thought about the food? Who asked you to be a restaurant critic?* Most likely, these self-proclaimed food critics completely missed out on the amazing education being shared, because they thought it was their job to criticize the food.

Who said you had to be a critic and have an opinion about *everything?* Unless your career is food or film critic, do you really need to be so demonstrative in letting everyone know what you think and feel about certain things? When you produce your own Broadway show, then you can critique Broadway. In the meantime, being nice doesn't mean just biting your tongue; it means choosing to let things go.

For me, a person who always interjects an opinion and critiques every little thing is coming from a place of ego. When I come from my insecure, low self-esteem, ego place, it's because I want you to feel good about *me.* And when anyone comes from that place, there's no room for another opinion. There's no room for you to feel good about yourself. I call it the "It's all about me" syndrome. Well, maybe I don't call it that, but I certainly know what it's like to be around.

Do you know people who, the older they get, the more critical they become? They have a blasted opinion about everything: "That's disgusting! That stinks! That's inappropriate!"

When I was coming up on my twenty-ninth birthday, I went to see a psychic who candidly told me that I was a serious old man at the ripe old age of twenty-eight. She said that if I didn't "lighten up" by the time I turned thirty, I'd live the rest of my life as a serious old man. I took her advice and asked some friends to teach me how to lighten up, relax, let things go, and have fun. I spent that year before my thirtieth birthday consciously and purposefully practicing what my friends taught me. I took a lot of weekend trips, went to outdoor concerts, had picnics, went camping, spent a lot of time with my young nieces and nephews, and did anything else that seemed spontaneous, simple, easy, and—in contrast to the serious businessman I'd become—irresponsible. Soon after I turned thirty, I "packaged" my newfound way of life and launched a speaking career. On my brand-new business cards, I fittingly had "Lighten Up" printed under my name, more as a reminder to myself than to others.

When people feel it's their role to be a critic—which easily bleeds into critiquing anything and everything—they miss out on simple pleasures, gifts, learning opportunities, adventures, discoveries, and growth. Critics miss out on life. Let go, lighten up, and you'll quickly see how much happier and fulfilling being nice can be.

Focusing on Too Many Issues

Keeping track of and managing "issues" can become a full-time job. It can occupy the majority of your thought processes while depleting valuable energy that you could be using to truly make a difference. Here's how it happens:

To be a good citizen and contribute to society, you begin to take on issues and causes. Your first concerns might be related to political, environmental, and economic issues. Then you move into issues related to human behavior and how people should treat each other. Sounds responsible and politically correct so far, doesn't it? Sure, but it doesn't end there. You then begin to take on the issues of which color your neighbors should paint their house, the appropriate length of a total stranger's hemline, and whether or not households three thousand miles away should be allowed to own more than two cats.

It's almost as if you move through life collecting as many issues as possible—as if you believe that "he who dies with the most issues wins." In reality, having so many issues will almost guarantee an early grave. Focusing on all those issues gets exhausting. It requires a great deal of time and energy to worry about all the things you can control, let alone the things you can't.

The challenge in having so many issues—so many things that don't work and keep you in a constant state of alarm—is that you don't have the time or energy to enjoy the things that do work. A good friend of mine refers to this as putting yourself in mental jail.

Let me give you some valuable, candid, useful, simple, silly, effective, "like I haven't heard that before" advice:

Let it go. Who cares? So what!
Build a bridge and get over it!

I believe there are many topics that need to become "non-issues." I would never attempt to dictate to a person what their non-issues should be; I can only decide upon my own. However, I challenge you and I challenge myself to be very clear as to which issues are important and worth standing up for, and which issues can become non-issues. It's great to have a mind of your own, but use it where it matters and choose your battles wisely. When you choose to let things go and make things non-issues, not only do you release other people to be who they are, you also set yourself free.

How can you decide which topics are issues and which ones are non-issues? A lovely, funny, and powerful motivational speaker by the name of Rita Davenport used to say, "If money can fix it, it's not a problem." By this definition, there are many things that bring you sorrow and misery, but if money can fix them, they're not a problem.

Although parents may spend hundreds of thousands of dollars on their sick child, money may not fix their little child's health issues. That's a genuine problem. Although governments may spend billions of dollars on security and defense, money cannot eliminate the hatred and racism in the world. Those are genuine problems.

Here's a simple exercise for sorting out your issues and non-issues. On a piece of paper, make a list of all the things that cause you to worry, lose sleep, and drag through life. Then, for each item on the list, ask yourself, "Can money fix this?" and write "yes" or "no" beside each item. Be aware of investing too much energy worrying about the things that money can fix. Save your strength for the no's on the list.

◪ Always Being Right

The annoying and unflattering side effect of people who always have to have an opinion and always have to be a critic is that they begin to believe they must be right about their opinions.

Have you ever been in an argument with someone you truly loved and cared about, and yet you just couldn't let go of your position? The issue may or may not have had much importance or merit, and you may or may not have been certain that your position was right, yet it was more important for you to be right and state your opinion, your case, your position, or your stance than to let it go and be nice. Even if there'd been a jury present to rule in your favor, proving that your side of the argument was right, please ask yourself the following question (from *A Course in Miracles*):

"Do you want to be right, or do you want to be happy?"

⬛ Always Finishing First

I facilitate a team-building activity called Shot-In-The-Arm, in which a group of people must get from one side of the room to the other while encountering physical obstacles along the way. Although the game doesn't end until *everyone* makes it across the finish line, it never fails that one or two individuals race out, ignoring the obstacles and pleas for help from their fellow team members, just so they can finish first.

Once, in a discussion that follows the exercise, a young woman shared with the group that she'd always been very goal oriented. She said that when the guidelines of the game were explained, all she heard was "Get to the other side." So she set out, and sure enough, she was the first person across the line. Once she crossed, though, she looked back and saw a whole group of people laughing, having fun, and getting to know each other—even though they hadn't crossed the finish line. She said to herself, "I crossed first, but look what I missed out on."

In this case, maybe nice guys do finish last, but they have more fun along the way. Life isn't always about being in a race and finishing first. Sometimes it's about the journey and the people you meet along the way. Nice guys help other people finish and enjoy the benefits of finishing together, or even finishing after everyone else. Mean guys who race to the finish miss out on all the fun.

⬛ Always Talking about Yourself

Another character trait that can diminish your nice factor is always talking about yourself. It's a bad habit to *not* be interested in what other people think, do, or feel. I say it's a bad habit because people who aren't interested in others have *trained* themselves to be this way, just as some people train themselves to be mean or to enjoy smoking. They're all bad habits, and bad habits can be broken.

Correcting this one is really simple. What's everyone's favorite subject? Themselves. If you want to let people know you're nice and that you have an interest in them, give them the opportunity to talk about themselves. How do you do that? Ask them. Simply say, "Tell me about *you*."

What if someone starts talking about a hobby that completely bores you to tears? Does that mean you're done, or that you have to pretend to be interested just to prove you're a nice person? Nope. For me, to understand other people and what makes them tick helps me to understand myself and what makes me tick. Being curious about human nature—why people think, believe, and act the way they do—helps me understand my own intricate physical, mental, and emotional control panels. To build your character, expand your horizons, learn new things, and increase your nice factor, you must break that old bad habit of being bored by others and instead learn how to be inquisitive, curious, and fascinated by them.

Let's say someone at a party tells you that their hobby is stamp collecting, and you feel that stamp collecting is the most boring hobby *ever*. Let's rehearse a script:

Q: Stamp collecting, huh? What first got you interested in that?

A: I had an uncle who was a stamp collector, and when he died he willed his collection to me.

Q: Where did your uncle grow up?

A: He grew up in Queens from the time he was eight years old.

Q: Where did he live before that?

A: He was a Jewish immigrant who came to the United States during World War II.

Q: Do you know much about his experiences then?

Instead of instantly ending the conversation, the skill here is to continue with a genuinely curious line of questions until you find something interesting. When that happens, you may suddenly look at this "boring" stamp collector and see the most remarkable person you've met in a long time.

You spent many years learning how to talk, write, and read. How many seminars have you attended on how to listen? Genuine listening means hearing with the intent to understand and get to know someone. If you do that, there's no way you could possibly finish last.

There's No Substitute for Being Nice

Have you ever met someone whose attitude seems to be, "I'll be nice until I get what I want"? It's kind of like the people who stay in shape until they get married, or the ones who hold in their gut when someone attractive walks by. They may think they're pulling a fast one, but no one is fooled for long. It's the same way with the following substitutes for being nice.

■ Being Rich Does Not Replace Being Nice

Why are some rich people mean and nasty? Because they can be. Money is a powerful thing to possess, and in most scenarios it will get you exactly what you want. A person without a lot of money would need to rely on other qualities, traits, or possessions—such as charm, personality, kindness, and niceties—to negotiate what they want in the world. But a rich person can do it with a snap of the fingers.

Be careful. Watch yourself. Be conscious of what the "perks" in life can do to deteriorate and weaken your nice factor. Be mindful of how you utilize the financial gifts you've been given and how your use of money makes other people feel about themselves.

I personally don't have a lot of wealthy friends or acquaintances, but I will say that the few I do have are wonderful examples for me on how to behave as a wealthy man. I was taught that if you despise rich people, you'll never be rich. Yes, I have a desire to be wealthy, and I feel that my attitude about money is quite healthy. You can do a lot of great things on this planet if you have a lot of money. As I share in an upcoming chapter, you need mentors to show you the way, even for becoming a responsible rich person.

One person who immediately comes to mind is a man by the name of John Paul DeJoria, the co-founder and CEO of the Paul Mitchell hair care company. I've watched John Paul in almost every type of scenario, from a hectic office to a board meeting, from dining out in a restaurant to dashing through a crowded airport, from hosting a small dinner party in his home to taking phone call after phone call. No matter what situation he's in, John Paul is always nice.

One such example of John Paul's niceness occurred the day I was in his Malibu home for a casual meeting with him. Before we began, John Paul explained that he was expecting an important phone call and asked if I'd mind if he left the phone on. "Of course not," I replied.

A few minutes into our meeting, the phone rang. John Paul apologized to me, and then answered the phone. As I sat there in close proximity (and eavesdropping range), it suddenly became apparent that John Paul was speaking to the president of the United States. In fact, to confirm my astonishment, I glanced at John Paul's assistant with an obvious question on my face, to which the assistant whispered, "Yep. It's *the* president." During their ten-minute phone call, John Paul was understandably kind, gracious, and nice; after all, it was the president.

The call ended, and John Paul and I went back to our meeting. A few minutes later, the phone rang again, and once again John Paul apologized to me for needing to take the call. Only this time it wasn't the president. It was a seamstress who was sewing a Halloween costume for one of John Paul's daughters. Their phone conversation lasted about ten minutes as well, but I was very aware of something pleasantly surprising: John Paul was just as kind, just as gracious, and just as nice to this seamstress as he was to the president of the United States.

◼ Having a PhD Does Not Replace Being Nice

Have you ever been around people who have multiple degrees from the College of Snobbery and who use their intelligence as a stick to beat up other people?

Education can do funny things to some people. You'd think education would help them live happier, more productive lives, and that their happiness would let them include other people. Yet for some, the more education, knowledge, and degrees they receive, the less confident they become of their abilities (which is where ego comes from).

You'd easily see a perfect example of this if you compared a group of adults to a kindergarten class filled with five-year-old children. If you asked the kids, "How many of you are really good at art?" how many hands do you think would go up? *All of them!* If you continued, "How many of you are really good at playing a musical instrument?" how many hands do you think you would see? Again, all of them. "How many of you are really good at acting in a play?" How many hands? *Every one.*

If you asked the same number of adults, "How many of you are really good at playing a musical instrument?" what would most likely happen? You'd see some blank stares, some yawns, and lots of squirming and fidgeting. Perhaps someone would respond with, "I took piano lessons for thirty-five years, but no, I'm just not good at playing the piano."

Where did we grown-ups lose our self-confidence? Little kids have it, but somewhere along the way, despite our education and mastery of new tasks and skills, we adults have diminished our soul's capacity for being able to confidently say, "Sure. I'm good at that, and so are you!" Unfortunately, when we lose our confidence in ourselves, we sometimes become less inclusive of others. We have so much to unlearn.

◧ Being Religious Does Not Replace Being Nice

We all know so-called religious people who use their religion as an excuse to belittle, judge, demean, and yes, as a stick to beat up other people. They think that attending church or synagogue on the weekends excuses them from being nice for the rest of the week. They especially feel as if they've been let off the hook of being nice toward those who don't have the same beliefs or practices as they. Oh, the tragedies, heartbreaks, and mistreatments that take place in the name of religion.

One of my favorite fables is about a man who has died and is standing at the gates of heaven, being judged by God. The man asks for forgiveness and pleads, "God, I tried to get into that church, but they wouldn't let me in." God responds, "You know, I've been trying to get into that church myself for years, and they won't let me in, either!"

Let me state it, simply and directly:

You can't be a bitch for God!

◧ Being Funny Does Not Replace Being Nice

Can you be funny and not be nice? Absolutely. I had a friend growing up who was always so funny and quick. His wit kept us in stitches. I loved being around him because he made me laugh. But as I got older, I experienced a relationship where another friend's sister was mentally challenged. All of a sudden my funny friend's humor regarding "retards" wasn't so funny anymore. I realized that his sense of humor was at someone else's expense, and his jokes were founded upon demeaning other people.

It May Not Be Illegal, But Is It Nice?

Oh, the ways in which we justify our actions. We live in a society that relies on lawmakers to tell us what behavior is acceptable and what behavior is not. We figure, "I didn't do anything illegal, so my actions are acceptable and justifiable, even if they weren't nice."

Yes, we want to make sure our actions don't violate the laws of the land, but we also have other laws to live by. There are laws of nature, laws of the mind, laws of the heart, laws of religion, and so on. There's also *karma*, which basically means you get what you deserve—and have you noticed that karma comes along a lot sooner than usual these days?

I don't know about you, but I figure that there are intelligences out there that have more power and wisdom than me, and that all these different laws exist for reasons I may never comprehend—nor do I need to in order to yield, and even surrender, to their existence and effect on me. To think that the only laws we have to live by are the ones written down in law books, while we ignore all others, is a frightening proposition. Being nice means we might also want to make sure we're in line with all the other sets of laws, because they *all* play their role.

Oxymorons

Before leaving this topic of the habits, traits, and characteristics of not-nice people, there's one more group I have to include. These are the professionals whose very job description requires them to be kind, caring, loving individuals. They're the people who probably chose careers in teaching, medicine, hairdressing, and service industries out of a sense of joy, love, and caring for people. But somewhere along the way they've lost that joy, they've gotten mean, and now they're sad examples of oxymorons in action.

▣ Mean Teachers

When a teacher is mean or comes from a place of ego, the doors of learning in the minds of students will slam shut. Being educated, humble, and nice are the greatest skills a gifted teacher could possess in order to facilitate the beautiful experience of learning.

▣ Mean Hairdressers

If you're like most people who frequent a beauty salon or spa, you'll probably agree that the main reason customers become loyal to their hairdressers is *not* just because they give great haircuts. In fact, there are many hairdressers who have awful technical abilities and give mediocre haircuts, yet they're booked for weeks and months in advance. Why? Because they're nice. They're fun. They make people feel welcome. They make people feel good about themselves, and their customers keep coming back for more.

◘ Mean Doctors and Nurses

The physical healing process for a patient is so delicate and requires so many different facets of wellness that to discard the importance of a nice, kindhearted doctor or nurse is tragic. Doctors and nurses especially must treat the whole person.

I am so inspired by City of Hope, whose dedicated physicians and researchers work tirelessly to find the causes of and cures for cancer and other life-threatening diseases. Since its founding in 1913, City of Hope has maintained a commitment to treating the whole person, not just the disease, by offering programs and services that go beyond what has traditionally been associated with hospital care. Their credo (as shown on their Web site, www.CityofHope.org) shows that they're driven by the following belief:

"There is no profit in curing the body, if in the process,
we destroy the soul."

If you want to be nasty, cruel, or unpleasant, then choose a career or activity where those traits might assist you, such as sumo wrestling or being a gossipy talk show guest. But don't become an oxymoron!

Nice Actions and Character Traits

Now that we've covered the not-nice habits, traits, and characteristics, let's look at the elements that create a nice person. Here are a few of the qualities and actions that go along with being nice.

◘ Patience

Years ago, my good friend Jimy Angel and I spent a week on the road together, sharing a hotel room while we did seminars. On the last day of our trip, after witnessing me jump out of bed when the alarm went off each morning and then do "laps" around the tiny hotel room as I got ready and organized myself for the day, Jimy said to me, "Winn, I have three words for you: RIT-A-LIN!"

I'm a very busy man. Who isn't these days? I also have a lot of energy, and I love lots of interaction with people. I love going to the gym with people, eating most of my meals out with people, and I'll even invite someone to walk out to my car with me if I have to go get something. I like to be with people a lot, and I don't require much alone time. Well, not everyone operates at the pace I do, and not everyone operates at the pace you do. If I want to be with people, then sometimes it has to be at their pace—I have to be patient. Patience for me is like it is for the little kid who's dragged along to go shopping with his mom, sitting outside a dressing room while she tries on outfit after outfit. It's pure torture. So here's what I do.

I have a day planner (I can't get into a handheld data system yet), which is constantly in my possession. That day planner is stuffed with all sorts of things: printed e-mails that I need to review; my scribblings about fun, new project ideas; photos of friends and family; photos of my favorite vacation spot; recent business cards I've collected; "love notes" from friends; magazine articles I tore out at home to read later; unopened mail; and over a hundred fortunes I've collected from Chinese fortune cookies. When I need to adjust my time to accommodate someone else's schedule, I have plenty to keep me busy and it's not so hard for me to be patient.

Laughter

It's a medical fact that stress, which is often caused by thoughts and beliefs, can lead to ulcers and other unfavorable physical calamities. In truth, it's not the stress that causes problems; it's the way you react to stress. Instead of letting stress make you ill, you can use laughter to help you heal. When you laugh and have fun, your body releases its own natural drugs called *endorphins*. These are the body's natural opiates—the ultimate "natural high." So for those of you who want to be nice and "play doctor," you can give others their daily dose of healthfulness through laughter.

Love

Of course the word *love* belongs in a book like this. Big surprise. However, in your pursuit to be nice, remember that *love* is a verb. It requires action. Hearing the words "I love you" is incredible and can send you soaring. The words alone can feel *so* good, both in hearing them and in saying them, but how wonderful it is when those words are accompanied by loving acts, thoughtful performances, and caring recitals.

I believe that love is a subject you can study. You can read books about it; listen to songs about it; attend seminars on it; and practice, practice, practice its curriculum in order to become a better representative of love's true meaning.

A much respected friend and mentor of mine, David Wagner, wrote a book titled *Life as a Daymaker: How to Change the World by Making Someone's Day*. His beautiful book details many examples of actions you can take to actively love your partner, your children, your grandchildren, a stranger, a co-worker, and yourself. I'm the type who loves to-do lists. Along with "Pick up a gallon of milk," you could add to your BE NICE to-do list, "Put a quarter in a gumball machine and walk away" or "Pick up lunch for someone at work you know is swamped"—both wonderful examples from David's book.

▣ Humor (Not at Someone Else's Expense)

Humor is such a wonderful skill and offering. Dr. Bernie Siegel, author of *Love, Medicine, and Miracles*, wrote that humor not only may have the potential to relieve pain directly, through endorphins and other physiological processes, it also diverts your attention and helps you relax. Humor can ease tension and lighten a situation. And when tension is low, niceness can flourish.

▣ Tolerance

It's amazing the little, tiny boxes we attempt to put people in. Our tolerance guidelines can become so limiting, and what we deem acceptable becomes so restrictive. I'm not sure of the source, but I love beliefs like "No one's special. Everyone's special," and Thomas A. Harris's concept of "I'm OK—You're OK."

How wonderful it would be if you were introduced to someone and your response following the description of this person was, "That's cool!" Here's an example of how that might look:

"Hey, this is my friend Nathan, who is _____."

(Fill in the blank, using descriptions such as Jewish, atheist, Mormon, Christian, Buddhist, gay, lesbian, Middle Eastern,

> *Southern, Mexican, a waiter, a recovering alcoholic, an attorney, a divorcee, an ex-convict, and so on.)*
>
> *Then remember, your response is, "That's cool!"*

When you practice being nice, everyone's descriptions will be totally and completely cool to you, because you tolerate and accept the masses.

▣ Humility

As you've already learned, a lack of confidence can lead to being egotistical. Humility is not a lack of confidence; it can exist on all levels of your confidence scale and in every facet of your ability, character, and personality.

To me, humility is the icing on the cake. It makes a physically attractive person a hundred times more attractive. Humility can never be counterfeit. It can only be genuine, and it can be learned. Yes, you can learn how to be humble, and the trait of humility is like the pied piper of nice people.

▣ ▣ ▣

If you saw yourself in any of the traits, attributes, and behaviors discussed in this chapter, and you discovered some areas in which you aren't nice, here's some great news: Anyone can *learn* to be nice, and the next chapter will get you started. Before you move on, here's one last thing I think you'll enjoy.

At the end of every chapter, you'll find a home-play assignment—a quick little exercise to jump-start your thinking and move you along on your BE NICE journey. Each one is short, sweet, and simple to complete. Are you ready? Here's your first one.

▣

Your Home-Play Assignment:

People Are _____

Find a tiny piece of scratch paper and something to write with. On the piece of scratch paper, write this down:

People are *interesting*
People are *strange*
People are *happy*

Fill in the three blank spaces after "People are" with three different adjectives. Quickly—write the first three words that pop into your head. Please make sure you do it without reading any further.

Now cross out "People are," and write "I am" in front of those three adjectives.

If you happen to have written something that wasn't so wonderful, please know that it does *not* represent the real you. It just suggests that you might have gotten off track somewhere along the way to being a nice person. Use your newfound knowledge to gain some insight as to what your personal home-play assignment might be—what you could work on. A list that contains negative traits is just the flip side to your true potential.

Who better to be a parent, the CEO of a big company, a stranger on an elevator, the coach of a Little League baseball team, a waitress, a lover, or a citizen of this planet than someone who wrote down, "People are wonderful, people are caring, people are nice"? If you're not quite there, you soon can be, and the next chapter will show you how.

Anyone Can Learn to Be Nice

"What we learn with pleasure we never forget."
—Louis Mercier

For years, I had the honor of traveling on the hair show circuit with a beautiful woman named Jeanne Braa, then artistic director of the Paul Mitchell hair care line. This wonderful friend and mentor of mine would challenge people to "practice being nice." That always confused me, because I used to believe the "nice gene" was something you either had or didn't have. It never occurred to me that you have to practice—that you have to consciously decide to learn and develop the necessary skills. I learned from Jeanne that being nice is not a physical trait passed on from your parents. It's not in your genes. It's not the same as being born with the heredity for growing six feet tall.

You aren't coded to be mean or to be nice. You can't get away with saying, "I'm just not nice. I was born that way, and there's nothing I can do about it." Being nice is something you learn. It's something you study. You have to practice for the rest of your life, and you will never graduate.

To be a brilliant pianist, you have to practice, practice, practice. To be in shape, you have to exercise regularly. You can't read one book or attend one seminar and think, *That's all I have to do.* That would be like going to aerobics one time and declaring, "I'm fit for life." If you wanted to be a brilliant hairdresser like Jeanne Braa, you wouldn't just pick up scissors and go knock on the door of a salon to get a job. You'd first have to enter a classroom and learn from the experts. If you wanted to be a doctor, you'd first have to enter a classroom and study a curriculum. Being nice requires the same process. It doesn't just come naturally. You have to learn from experts, and you have to study a curriculum.

Being nice is an ongoing, lifelong course. You never get to stop learning what it means and what it takes to be nice. But it's well worth the effort, because being nice can bring you rewards you never imagined. So, how do you learn to be nice? Keep reading, because that's what this chapter is all about.

Being Nice Brings Happiness

For my entire life, being happy has never come naturally to me. Happiness seems to come naturally to some people, but not to me, and that used to really upset me. I used to think, *I've read enough books and I've been to enough seminars on happiness and self-esteem. Why can't I just coast once in a while?* Well, I can't. I've learned that there are certain things I have to do every single day in order to be happy. I now know what those things are, I do them all the time, and I'm one of the happiest people I know.

A big part of my curriculum to become happy was to be nice. Be nice. Be nice. BE NICE! To become happy, I practiced being nice, and being nice brought about happiness beyond my utmost fantasies.

Joy and Pain Are Your Friends

There are two emotions that motivate people: One is joy, and the other is pain. You do something because you believe it will bring you joy, or you avoid it because you believe it will be painful or because you find yourself in pain and are motivated to do whatever it takes to get out of that pain. This is a very simple principle taught beautifully and effectively by mentors like Tony Robbins.

Why is this concept so important? Because if you attach pain to the idea of being nice, your heart and mind will reject the idea. If you believe that being nice will be painful because it means giving away your power, or letting people walk all over you, you'll reject any nudge to be a nice person. Similarly, if you attach joy to being nasty and mean—because you believe those behaviors show your power, your humor, and your take-control strength—then this entire book will seem juvenile and unimportant.

To begin your BE NICE journey, here's what you've got to do: You *must* attach joy to being nice. You must believe that being nice will ultimately help you get what you want and need. If you don't believe it, at least believe that I believe it. You must start to see how your very simple acts of being nice, even toward total strangers, can and do have a major impact on them, and even more so on you. You must start to experience the joy of letting people just be, see how much easier it is to let certain things go, and make certain issues non-issues. Eventually, you'll start to see how much pain, energy, and work are involved in taking the opposite approach.

This book is probably not the first time you've read the statement that life is a choice. You *choose* to find joy in certain things, and you *choose* to find pain in other things. Be careful which choices you make.

How Do You Eat an Elephant?

How do you start to believe all this? How do these simple ideas become second nature, comfortable habits, and a joyful way of life? As the old saying goes, one bite at a time. You don't have to save the world today. You don't have to be nice to everyone all at once. Why don't you start by just being nice to *really nice people?* Why don't you start with a kind word to a sweet old lady, and see how she responds? Take some baby steps here, and begin with people you *know* will react positively to your gifts of being nice. You can worry about taking on the nasty, bitter ones later.

"I Was Nice, and All I Got Was This Lousy T-Shirt! "

Sometimes you're nice to someone and they respond back with ignorance, meanness, indifference, boredom, or no response whatsoever. You say hello to total strangers and they look at you as though you're an axe murderer.

Being nice to people is not necessarily about the other person. You can be nice for selfish reasons—selfish in a good way. You can be nice out of your own self-interest.

When you're mean and you attack other people with your words, actions, or thoughts on a continual basis, there's a very good chance that you also "attack" yourself. A self-attack can have many faces, including addictions, eating disorders, disease, and negative self-talk like the following:

> *I'm so clumsy. I'm so fat. I'm so stupid.*
> *I'm a bad person. I'll never amount to much.*

When you choose to be nice to others, you begin to respect yourself, be nice to yourself, and show love to yourself to the same degree. Other people are your home-play assignments to improve your own self-worth and self-love.

Putting Your Best "Niceness" Forward

You could be a nice person, but if you don't let people see, know, and believe that you're nice, their perception might be that you're not. You have to learn how to "market" your niceness.

> *Why do I have to go out of my way to let people know I'm nice?*
> *Can't I just be who I am, and express myself freely?*
> *If they can't see that I'm a nice person, then that's their problem!*

In so many areas of life, most of us try to put our best foot forward. We market ourselves so people will want to get to know us better.

A woman may be beautiful on the inside, but she'll still put on make-up every day to make herself look more beautiful on the outside. Why? So people will look at her, want to get to know her, and eventually see her inner beauty.

A man may have a loud voice, which might be perceived as mean-ness. To counteract that perception, he may "disguise" his voice or pur-posely speak more softly so people aren't offended by his loudness and will eventually get to know him and see that he's a nice person.

Another person might be well read, well educated, and well traveled, with a great deal of insight and experience about all sorts of topics and interests. A conversation with that person could prove to be fascinating, entertaining, and enlightening. But unless the person is first perceived as nice, that same conversation could be perceived as overbearing, insensitive, nonstop dialogue and chatter. For some reason, when you know people are nice, you become much more interested in what they have to say.

You go through life studying a variety of curriculums: art, history, language, hobbies, sports, astrology, and so on. If you're mean and an expert in anything, not too many people will care about what you know. But if you're a lifelong student of the curriculum of being nice, your knowledge in any other subject becomes alluring. Put your niceness before and above everything else, and all of a sudden you become a fascinating individual whom others want to get to know.

Be a Nice-Master

Being nice requires you to become a nice-master, which requires a full range of emotions. Why? Simply because if you want to have an overall reputation among any and all types of people for being nice, you'll need to relate to any and all types of people. Since human beings have a full range of emotions, you'll need a full range of emotions and a myriad of ways for dealing with and relating to them. How can you be perceived as a nice person to someone who loves to laugh if you rarely experience laughter yourself? How can you relate to a person who feels emotions deeply if you rarely experience emotions deeply yourself? For me, a wonderfully full day is when I can experience it all—laughter, sadness, caring, vulnerability, adventure, and a good cry. (To me, that all happens in just one episode of *The Golden Girls*.)

When it comes to mastering some things in life, including being nice, there are no quick fixes. As I've shared over and over again, being nice is a lifelong study and practice. But just as a shot of penicillin can quickly make a sick person feel better, a shot of any of the following practices can help you feel better and place you on your path to becoming nice.

◪ Sing Songs at Full Volume in Your Car

Record a tape or CD of songs that can instantly put you in a good mood. Play that tape or CD whenever you need a little dose of cheering up or a reminder of simple, nice things. My homemade BE NICE tape includes "Greatest Love of All" by Whitney Houston, "Watershed" by the Indigo Girls, "One" by Elton John, and "Where Is the Love" by Black Eyed Peas.

◻ Repeat "Nice Mantras" 100 Times a Day

My mantra for the past several years has been "Thank you, God." Whenever I see a wonderful sunset, I either silently or out loud say, "Thank you, God." If I have a great dinner conversation with a good friend, or a surge of bliss runs through my body for no apparent reason, I simply say, "Thank you, God."

To remind yourself to use your nice mantra often, write it on several three-by-five-inch cards and place them visibly where you'll see them often, such as on your bathroom mirror, your refrigerator, your office desk, or your car dashboard.

◻ Send Lots of Love Notes and Cards

Find opportunities to show gratitude and to express your love and friendship by sending handwritten notes and cards to family, friends, and new acquaintances. Keep a box of cards on your desk or in a convenient spot where you'll see it often. Make it a good habit to spend a couple of minutes several times per week expressing gratitude through the lost art of handwritten love notes.

◻ Perform Random Acts of Kindness

I watched an *Oprah* show years ago titled something like "Random Acts of Kindness." As only Oprah can, she shared many examples and stories of these random, thoughtful acts, including one that I've performed many times since then: paying for the car behind me when going through a toll booth. When my nice factor is low and I want to give it a boost, you'll find me frantically looking for a toll road somewhere. It works every time.

◻ Develop the Language of a Nice Person

I love it when total strangers, such as a waiter or waitress, call me "sweetheart" or "darling." It's a gift they give to me, and it's an easy one to pass along.

It's Got to Be Fun

Why do we think that the process of improving ourselves in any area is supposed to be a chore? For example, we make New Year's resolutions and begrudgingly claim, "I have to lose weight." If it's drudgery, will we stick with it? No. It's got to be fun.

If I'm not having fun with something, I'm the type of person who won't do it much longer. I'm not saying I won't do it for another year—if something isn't fun, I won't do it for another *day*.

How do you make things fun? Follow these two steps:

1.   Find mentors and gurus for the area you want to improve.

2.   Find people who want to play with you.

Step 1: Find Mentors

None of us would be where we are today, in terms of our happiness or success, if it weren't for role models and examples who've guided us and shown us the way. We can't learn everything through firsthand experience; it takes too long, and the pain and sacrifice to learn every lesson would be too great. A wise person learns from *other people's experiences*. We call those people "mentors."

For the most part, mentors are people who've achieved a bit of success in their own lives, financial or otherwise. They've usually had to overcome certain obstacles or hardships, and it's because of those hardships—and the fact that they overcame them—that they have something to share and that we want to listen. We're inspired when we see someone who's overcome the same hardships we struggle with; they give us hope.

When it comes to mentors, masters, and artists, I don't believe that God plays favorites. I don't believe God gives more potential to one person than to another. Believing that gives me hope because I tell myself, "If they did it, then so can I."

I also don't believe that one mentor could encompass all talents and all wisdom in the areas we need to learn about in order to achieve balance and happiness in our lives. We need different mentors for different lessons.

In interviewing people for my *Masters* Audio Club program, I've recorded some amazing histories and stories. Trevor Sorbie, one of the world's leading hairdressers, told us that after receiving the British Hairdresser of the Year award for the second time, he ended up in the hospital with severe depression and truly believed he'd never work again. Somehow he overcame that, went on to build an empire, and has received that same award two more times. Now, for me, that was inspiring, because I've always had to work hard on my own happiness. If he can do it, I can do it, too.

Jeanne Braa, whom you met at the beginning of this chapter, told us in her *Masters* Audio Club interview that she was so poor as a single mother working in a Montana salon, that she had to take in sewing at night just to make ends meet. When she wanted to meet hair care pioneer Paul Mitchell, she actually took out a loan on her sewing machine to buy a plane ticket to go hear him speak. She is now a beautiful, successful, and legendary hairdresser.

Joe L. Dudley, Sr., president of Dudley Products Inc., told us in his *Masters* interview that at the age of five he was labeled mentally retarded. It wasn't until years later, when his girlfriend told him she wouldn't marry him because she didn't want to have stupid children, that he finally decided to get an education. He went on to earn a PhD; has met with three sitting presidents, including Nelson Mandela, then president of South Africa; and is now one of the largest manufacturers and distributors of ethnic hair care products in the world.

Van Council, owner of Van Michael Salons, a very successful salon chain based in Atlanta, has had a speech impediment his whole life. Coupled with his Southern accent, nobody could understand what he was saying—they all thought he was foreign. He decided to use that to his advantage, figuring that a "foreigner" could charge $100 for his haircuts. He charges $150, and his three Atlanta salons do a total business of $14 million a year.

As you can see, I look to mentors within my own industry, because that helps me in my business, both financially and to stay in love with my industry. I also look to mentors outside my industry, to people I know personally and those I've never met.

At age sixteen, Angie Cranor survived a terrible car accident that left her paralyzed from the waist down. One night while lying in her hospital bed, Angie realized she had a decision to make. She had to decide whether she was going to get bitter or get *better*. She chose to get better and has been a wonderful mentor to me and to thousands by preaching things like, "If your dream is big enough, the facts won't matter. Always remember that you can do anything you want, no matter how big the obstacles may appear. The accident wasn't a bad thing. It was just a difficult thing that has made my life better." Angie is amazing.

Diagnosed with cancer, bestselling author Louise Hay decided to put her money where her mouth was. She'd written about mental patterns, and she firmly believed that mental healing worked. She took responsibility for her own healing, reading about and studying every alternative therapy she could find, and she applied many of them to her own care. Six months after her original diagnosis, she was declared cancer free.

In October 1996, cyclist Lance Armstrong was diagnosed with advanced testicular cancer that had spread to his lungs and brain. Through a combination of surgery, chemotherapy, and an unbelievably inspiring attitude, he became the first American—and only the second person in the world—to win five consecutive victories in the grueling, twenty-three-day, 2,125-mile Tour de France.

Choose Nice-Mentors

As you can see, I have many nice-mentors because it felt natural for me to seek them out. Even as a child, I loved nice characters in movies who did nice things—Julie Andrews' character in *The Sound of Music* comes to mind, as well as Mary Poppins, also played by Julie Andrews. (Maybe I just like Julie Andrews!)

We're all drawn to certain heroes, celebrities, supermodels, or sports figures who exemplify our different hobbies and interests. If you're *not* naturally drawn to nice-mentors, you'll need to find and choose some. You wouldn't choose a mean, abusive, lawbreaking sports jock to be your spiritual mentor, and you shouldn't choose anyone but nice people to be your nice-mentors.

For me, little kids are *huge* mentors, simply because they can teach me what I most need to know and practice, which is to have more fun in life. Not only do I make a conscious effort to hang out with my young nieces and nephews for the mentoring, I also enjoy it. I have plenty of serious adults all around me who want to have serious, adult, all-about-business conversations, so my personal growth and happiness don't require more of that. I need to lighten up. I need to be silly and irresponsible. I need to find fun and pleasure in simple things. Little kids know how to do that, and they do it naturally.

Now, here's where it gets monumental: When I spend time with my young nieces and nephews, I'm not dragging them into my world, I'm losing myself in *their* world. I'm not forcing them to sit still in a formal restaurant and act like proper young ladies or gentlemen, I'm allowing them to drag me outside the restaurant to run around on the grass and play whatever silly game they invent.

Another one of my nice-mentors came right from my own industry and happens to be a Catholic nun by the name of Sister Bonnie Steinlage, SFP, a Franciscan Sister of the Poor. (Okay, so I took this nice thing to the extreme—I need a lot of help and mentoring, so I chose a nun.) Sister Bonnie decided many years ago that she wanted to become a hairdresser, as a Catholic nun, and do hair for the homeless. She graduated from beauty school and opened her own little business. It was located in the tiny bathroom of the Mary Magdalene House, a shower facility for the homeless in downtown Cincinnati. For seven years, Sister Bonnie cut hair for ten thousand homeless people in that tiny bathroom, until a group of amazing individuals eventually built a wonderful salon for her and the homeless.

I had the chance to fly to Cincinnati and spend time with Sister Bonnie to interview her for my *Masters* program. In that interview, she said, "I'm the only Catholic nun who can say I've been in the bathroom with ten thousand men, and they all came out smiling!" I love her commitment, which is packaged and even marketed with humor. Her purpose is to do good work, but she doesn't beat people over the head with it. Instead, she draws support for her cause by using humor, by not taking herself too seriously, and by making people feel comfortable about supporting the homeless. Now, that's a mentor.

At the end of her *Masters* interview, Sister Bonnie said, "My clients happen to be homeless, so of course they don't pay me anything for my services. Perhaps your clients are paying you ten dollars or a hundred dollars, but they're homeless on the inside."

Now, how does all that add up to me choosing Sister Bonnie as a nice-mentor? Well, homelessness can frighten and confuse people—I know that it does me. I used to have a difficult time seeing beyond the dirty exterior of the homeless, and I could easily jump into judgment about how those people ended up in the position they're in. Is that the person I want to be? No, hence my need for a nice-mentor like Sister Bonnie.

After I spent time with her, talked about her in my seminars, and helped raise money for her organization, her lovely mentoring finally started to seep in.

One day, I arrived at one of my schools and found a homeless man hanging out in front of the building. Normally, because of my own fears and prejudices, I would've ignored him. Or worse, I would've called the police to have him removed. But because of Sister Bonnie's influence on me, I chose a different plan. I decided to step outside of my own egotistical, fear-driven self and began talking to him. After a ten-minute conversation about who knows what, I asked him if he'd like to come into the school for a service, to which he enthusiastically replied, "Yes!" I escorted him in, had him take a seat in the reception area, then walked to the back of the school and asked a group of students, "Who wants to be a daymaker?" Ten students immediately raised their hands. I grabbed one of them, brought him to the reception area, introduced him to the homeless man, and asked him to take good care of his "client." Two hours later, after being shampooed, conditioned, groomed, and cared for, the homeless man left the school.

I won't attempt to exaggerate or embellish the story by talking about how the experience changed the homeless man's life, because I honestly don't know how it affected him. His experience is not the point. The person who changed was me. First of all, how difficult was it for me to offer this man a service in my school? How much did it actually cost me? Not much, but that's also not the point of this story.

The point is this: Because of Sister Bonnie's simple mentoring, I made a little, tiny shift in my thinking and perception about the homeless. I haven't gone on to raise millions of dollars for homelessness, and I haven't volunteered hundreds of hours to help that cause. But I did let go of a fear and a belief system that didn't serve me and had held me back from feeling good about myself. Finding and studying a new program that will make you happy is all about tiny shifts in thought and action, which eventually add up to monumental strides of growth. Nice-mentors can nudge you along that path.

Step 2: Find People Who Want to Play with You

The second step in making things fun is to find people who want to "play" with you in the area in which you're trying to improve. Having partners and friends who also want to improve themselves in the same area gives you hope, keeps you focused and motivated, and makes the process fun.

For example, just because you may not enjoy going to the gym to exercise doesn't mean you have the option of not going, but you do have the option of making it fun. How? Well, you might try finding one or two people who want to go with you—the more the merrier—and turning gym time into social time as well. On those days when one of you is not motivated to go, the other person will drag you along.

Little kids are brilliant at finding people to play with. They'll go up to a total stranger and say, "Hi! Wanna be my friend?" As adults, we've somehow lost that ability. We waste so much time and energy screaming, "Why don't you want to be my friend?" We work so hard trying to convince people who don't want to play with us, who don't want to support us, that we completely fail to notice those people standing on our sidelines yelling, "Choose me! Choose me!"

Hey, it's tough out there, and there are a lot of people who can't wait to rain on your parade and scoff at your silly notion of learning to be nice. Oftentimes, those naysayers are louder than the loving, supportive people who believe strongly in your BE NICE curriculum. Don't let their voices drown out the rest. Just keep searching, and you're sure to find supportive people who want to study, practice, and play with you in your BE NICE journey.

SW, SW, SW!

As you attempt to find people who want to play with you, please remember the philosophy of SW, SW, SW! It stands for,

Some will, some won't, so what!

Perhaps there are people in your life who don't want to go to the gym with you, or who don't want to do volunteer work. They say they don't want to go to a seminar or enroll in a course because they already know it all. Even worse, they'll try to discourage you by telling you it won't do you any good or you're just wasting your time. Ignore those people. Move on. Find someone who will go with you and is excited about what you're excited about. Remember: *Some will, some won't, so what!*

You Attract What You Value

One of my favorite movies was *Field of Dreams*. Its main line and message was "Build it and they will come." If you want to live your life filled with kind, nice people, then build a life that will attract those types of people. If you've chosen to divorce yourself from negative, garbage programming, and have instead chosen to value positive, nice people, then that's who you'll attract.

People who are bitter, mean, or judgmental don't even know I exist. It never fails that on a plane I get seated next to the nicest people.

I once landed at the Chicago airport and was waiting for a taxi in very cold weather. Because I sell audiotapes at my seminars, I was traveling with two large boxes of tapes, along with my very large suitcase. After standing in the taxi line for over forty-five minutes, cold and tired, it was finally my turn. Believe it or not, two taxi drivers pulled up, opened their trunks, took one look at my "load," and turned me down. I was furious. Finally a third taxi pulled up. The driver jumped right out, happily loaded my three big pieces into his trunk, opened the door for me to jump in, and away we sped toward my hotel.

During the drive, my thoughts were still stuck back at that cold curb, upset about those first two drivers. Somehow the kindness of my driver's voice pierced through my pity-party anger and I began hearing about his lovely family, his native country, and his plans to move to Boston to study medicine. He asked if I'd ever been to Boston, to which I replied that I had and that it was one of my favorite cities. He then asked, "Are people nice in Boston?"

Right then, I realized what had happened to me back at that cold airport curb, waiting for this third taxi to come along. I'd been turned down by two drivers who perhaps weren't nice people so that I could have the gift of this very nice man. With a "boy am I silly" grin on my face, I replied to my driver, "Yes, there are lots of nice people in Boston, and you'll attract them all."

I truly believe that we attract what we value and focus upon. If you value and invest in people because of a certain trait or quality, then you very well could attract people who possess that trait or quality. If you value looks, wealth, power, or celebrity over being nice, then be prepared to attract people who have those attributes but may not be nice. I'm not saying that beautiful, wealthy, powerful, and famous people aren't nice, but make sure you value other things as part of the package, including the character trait of being nice. If you constantly seek out and acknowledge nice people, then spiteful people won't even know you exist. I'm thinking that those two taxi drivers who turned me down hadn't even seen me standing on that cold curb—and that turned out to be a good thing.

Be Approachable

As part of my own curriculum and practice to be nice, whenever I traveled and was running through airport after airport, I used to wear a T-shirt that said, WHATEVER THE QUESTION, LOVE IS THE ANSWER. I wore that shirt because its message made people feel like they had permission to approach me. They assumed that only a nice guy would wear a shirt like that, and they felt comfortable smiling at me or even chatting with me. I loved it because even though I was on the road alone, I felt as though I made many connections with some very nice people.

I don't have that shirt anymore, but I now have BE NICE tattooed on my upper arm. About the only time the tattoo is visible is when I'm at the gym. How do people respond? The same way as when I wore that T-shirt. I get lots of smiles, friendly nods, and many people who come up and begin a conversation about my tattoo. That's cool. I'm approachable, and I wouldn't have it any other way.

■ ■ ■

I need a lot of nice people in my life to remind me to be nice, and being approachable is one way to make sure I find them. This next home-play assignment is a great way to find nice-mentors to help you on your journey of learning to be nice.

Your Home-Play Assignment:

Who Are Your Nice-Mentors?

My parents have been happily, romantically married for sixty years. They're my mentors. If they can maintain a long-term, happy relationship, then so can I. They're not rich, they're not famous, but they're my mentors. Who are yours?

If you haven't already identified your mentors, or if you'd like to add to your list, here's a home-play assignment to make it easy. I challenge you to find your mentors, not just for business, but for every area of your life. Find mentors for your physical growth, your creative development, your business progress, your emotional maturity, and so on.

Make a list of the family members, friends, and acquaintances who:

1. Make you laugh – *Jamie, Tyler, Alana*
2. Make you feel humble –
3. Make you feel grateful – *God*
4. Make you feel thoughtful, pensive, and reflective – *Some Clients of mine*
5. Make you feel and act silly or childlike – *my Kids*

The people you've listed will become your mentors to help you develop your full range of emotions. Hang out with them. Study them. Watch them closely with an inquisitive and curious mind. Mirror their emotions and actions, even if it feels unnatural and silly to do so. Let them take the lead in deciding where you'll eat dinner or how you'll spend the day. You already know plenty about *you,* so for now put *you* aside as the main topic of conversation. Ask these newfound mentors questions about themselves and their feelings. After all, what's everyone's favorite subject? Themselves.

Ask your nice-mentors questions about what you observe and experience while you're with them. People love to talk about their feelings, their beliefs, their opinions and insights, or their description of the meaning of life. As you learn how to ask great questions, you'll receive great answers and therefore great insights. You'll begin to experience something different, and from those experiences you begin to create different actions, new and different habits, and a better character and personality. You become multifaceted, and *that,* my friend, makes you more interesting, attractive, and approachable.

chapter 3

First, Be Nice to Yourself

"People often say that this or that person has not yet found himself.
But the self is not something one finds; it is something one creates."
—Thomas Szasz

Simply put, you can't give what you don't have. It's difficult to be nice to others when you're not nice to yourself. And it's difficult to be nice to yourself when you don't feel good about yourself. If you think this sounds simple, harsh, complex, or like a lot of work, you're right. Working on yourself and cultivating your own self-esteem *is* a lot of work. It's a full-time job. You'll never receive your final certificate of graduation and be told it's time to stop working on your self-esteem. You'll never arrive at a point in life when you make the announcement, "I have plenty of happiness and self-esteem. No more, thank you."

As I've said several times in earlier chapters, those individuals who have a difficult time being nice to others often come from a place of ego or a lack of self-esteem. Good self-esteem has nothing to do with ego; ego is the sign of insecurity. Here's how you know the difference. When you're in the presence of someone who's coming from a place of ego, they want you to feel good about whom? About them. But when you're in the presence of someone who feels good about themselves, they want you to feel good about yourself. In fact, you do feel good about yourself when you're with someone who has good self-esteem and loves themselves. Good self-esteem is a gift you give to others.

So, how do you give it if you don't have it? And how do you have it if you don't give it? Sometimes you just have to fake it till you make it. You simply start being nice to yourself, whether you think you deserve it or not. You fake it until you begin to believe, and the ideas in this chapter will help you get started.

Fall Back in Love

Here's a radical challenge: Make it a goal to fall back in love with yourself. When I give that challenge to a roomful of people in my seminars, I usually hear lots of nervous little giggles. For some reason, even the thought of "falling in love with me" seems extreme, and people reject the validity of the notion.

Why would you want to make it a goal, and eventually a reality, to fall back in love with yourself? Once again, this book is about seeking and sharing happiness, joy, purpose, and fulfillment. To offer those gifts to others, you first have to own them yourself. Again, at the risk of sounding redundant, you can't give what you don't have.

I once had the honor of knowing a wonderful woman named Noel DeCaprio. The owner of the Noelle Spa for Beauty and Wellness, she was quite successful in her career and business, and she was heralded by many as a mentor and leader within her industry. She'd been featured and interviewed in magazines and on television for her wisdom, and many people looked to Noel for coaching, her business ideas, and her "you can do it" approach.

Noel had also experienced a fourteen-year battle with breast cancer, which eventually took her life in December 1998. I interviewed Noel for an audiotape to raise money for breast cancer research at City of Hope's National Medical Center six months before her passing. In that interview, she shared that after her double mastectomy and months of chemotherapy, she looked in the mirror and hated herself. As she beheld the massive scarring and her bald head, she felt embarrassed by the fact that cancer could show up in her body, and she despised herself for it.

Now remember, Noel was a mentor to many people. They looked to her for inspiration, yet when she looked in the mirror, she hated herself. Noel was wise enough to know she had to find a way to fall back in love with herself, and she did it by making bathing a ritual. Every day, she'd spend hours in the ritual of bathing. She focused on the bath salts, the candles, the oils and creams, and the aromas. She'd spend time visiting little boutiques that sold such items, and even though she was buying them for herself, she'd have the store gift wrap everything. She put so much time into something that she'd never before had the time for—something that seemed so selfish and narcissistic—that eventually one day she woke up and realized she was back in love with herself.

Once Noel fell back in love with herself, she told her family, friends, and staff, "Tell everyone I have cancer. I'm out of the closet, and I want everyone to know so I can help as many people as I can." Noel told a wonderful little story about preparing to go out to a fundraising dinner, placing her scarf on her bald head, and still feeling a little unsure of herself. Her adorable and supportive husband Peter looked at her and said, "Now you go out there and show them how to have cancer!"

How Noel went on to raise money and awareness for cancer was unbelievable. But let me ask you: Could she have accomplished so much, and benefited so many people, had she not fallen back in love with herself?

Go through the Motions

To build your own gifts of happiness, joy, purpose, and fulfillment so you can offer them to others, and then validate more of those gifts for yourself, sometimes you might have to go through the motions of offering yourself gifts that you don't believe you deserve.

If you knew your lover had had a bad day, you'd want to do something about it, wouldn't you? Knowing that he or she was coming home from work, you might draw a nice bath, light candles around the bathtub, and place special salts or oils in the bathwater. Maybe you'd put on some soft music, turn down the lights, and turn the telephone ringer to "off." You'd then greet your lover boy or lover girl at the door to grab their briefcase or purse, hand them a glass of wine, and send them in to take a well-deserved, melt-your-stress-away, long, relaxing bath. You'd do that for a lover, but when was the last time you did it for yourself? When was the last time you treated yourself with such respect and love?

My challenge for you and for myself is to just go through the motions. Tonight, you might be sitting in that bathwater thinking, *What the hell am I doing here?* That's okay. Eventually, actions become habits, and habits become part of your personality, which builds your character and turns you into the type of person you were always meant to be, filled with blissful happiness and purpose.

Refill Your Reservoir

Cup your two hands together as though you were going to splash water on your face. Your two hands together represent your reservoir. Your reservoir is filled with everything that makes you who you are, everything that makes you wonderful. Your reservoir contains your dreams, your fantasies, your personality, your passion, your talents, and your skills. Do you ever feel at the end of the day that your reservoir is drained and empty? How does it get drained? Traffic. Bad weather. A new computer system at work. Your boss's bad mood.

How do you fill your reservoir back up? You could have it filled by having a customer or a friend send you a dozen roses, but can you count on that? You have to know how to fill your own reservoir. And by the way, what works for someone else may not work for you. One of your missions in life is to find out what fills up your own reservoir.

For me, my reservoir gets filled with a wonderful dinner out with a dear friend or two, in a small, quaint restaurant, with a bottle of wine and great conversation. That fills up my reservoir like you wouldn't believe. I bet I spend more money doing that than I spend on buying clothes or taking vacations. Also, for me, going to the gym with my best buddies will fill up my reservoir. There's something amazing about doing something that's so good for me and motivating someone I care about to do something good for them, too. And don't even get me started on how fabulous the conversations are between our sets of exercises.

The bottom line is that you have to make sure your needs are met, and sometimes the best way to make that happen is to meet them yourself.

Take Control of Your Life

Think for a moment about how a computer works. It's programmed to run specific functions and tasks. Its software determines the type of output and information it will provide, and it relies on the information or input received. When the computer receives good or accurate input, it performs well. When the computer receives inaccurate or "garbage" information, it gives back unusable, garbage information. This is known as "garbage in, garbage out," or GIGO.

Your mind is similar to computer software. The quality of the information you allow into your brain directly affects your thinking, beliefs, and behavior. What happens when you feed your mind garbage, focus on negative things, or surround yourself with negative people? What happens when you focus on violence and gossip? You probably tend to become worried, irritated, and tired. On the flip side, when you focus on the positive and productive things in your life, don't you tend to feel motivated, optimistic, and more energetic? What you focus on can affect your mood.

See if you agree with the following statements:

What I focus on is up to me.

*I have control over what I think about and
what I program into my mind.*

*When I focus on things that are distracting or negative,
my beliefs begin to change and my behavior is affected.*

If you agree with these statements, I'd like to suggest a three-step process to begin taking control of your life in order to be nice to yourself:

1. Eliminate and cancel negative programming

2. Create a new program of things that make you happy

3. Choose your focus

Step 1: Eliminate and Cancel Negative Programming

One of the most important things you can do to be nice to yourself is to eliminate things in your life that block or blur your perception of what being nice is all about. Divorce yourself from the people, beliefs, and experiences that cause you to be mean, unfeeling, and insensitive. Divorce yourself from even the subtleties of negative training.

People would love to assume that they'd never program garbage into their own minds, yet it often happens by default. By not being aware of the information you take in, you allow others to decide your programming. Maybe you allow the producers of one of those horrible, gossipy talk shows to decide what your programming will be, and since their choice for you is negative drama, that's what your mind, heart, and soul take in. Then your beliefs, your relationships, and your view of the entire planet are all about negative, hopeless drama.

If you love negative drama, you'll definitely attract dramatic, negative people who can't wait to tell you how bad their lives are, and who did what mean thing to whom.

Years ago a lovely woman who works for me would make it almost a daily ritual to tell me about all the negative drama and complaints from people at my business. She'd tell me, "This one said this, and that one said that." She truly believed she was doing me a favor by bringing me this negative information, and I think she thought it was a compliment that people would come to her with their problems and complaints.

Finally, one day I asked her, "Why are you so available for that type of information?" She looked at me with a puzzled expression, so I repeated, "Why do so many people want to dump all their negative drama onto you? Why are you available for that?" After a long conversation and a reminder about our company's very effective and positive system for expressing grievances, she finally realized she was *not* helping the individuals work out their problems, she was *not* bringing me information I could do anything with, and she was instead bringing stress and bitterness upon herself and her co-workers. This lovely woman is now no longer available for negative gossip and drama.

Have you ever had lunch with friends who had nothing to share but tragic stories they'd read in the news: "Did you hear about the guy who embezzled a million dollars from his company?" "Did you hear about that camper who got attacked by a bear?" I always want to ask them, "Do you know these people?" If the guy who lost the embezzled money or the guy who was attacked by the bear is *not* a member of your family, a friend, or an acquaintance, then why do you care?

Why do you want to invest so much time and energy into another person's misery? Why do you rubberneck to see accidents on the freeway? Why are gossip and dirt so interesting? Why is someone's misfortune so entertaining? Why don't simple acts of kindness inspire you? Why do stories of the good things people do bore you? When did you stop being a believer? We call it "reality TV," but why isn't niceness just as much a reality as a show like *Animals Who Attack?*

People are so willing to give credence and attention to negative stories, but they shrug off the positive ones. Remember the movie *Oh, God!* in which George Burns played the title role? God's goal was to use Jerry Landers, a simple grocery store manager played by John Denver, as his messenger to send hope to the world. God asked Jerry to contact the local newspaper and television station to deliver his message of hope, but no one believed that God had spoken to Jerry and wanted to deliver a message through him. At the end of the movie, God gave this speech in a courtroom:

> What about all that hoo-ha with the devil a while ago from that movie? Nobody had any trouble believing that the devil took over and existed in a little girl. All she had to do was wet the rug, throw up some pea soup, and everybody believed. The devil you could believe, but not God? . . .

> I'm not about to go around to every person in the world and say, "Look, it's me. I want to talk to you." So I picked one man— one very good man. I told him, God lives. I live. He had trouble believing, too, in the beginning. . . .

> I know how hard it is in these times to have faith, but maybe if you could have the faith to start with, maybe the times would change. You could change them. Think about it. Try. And try not to hurt each other. There's been enough of that, and it really gets in the way.

If you want to be nice, you must stop giving so much power and attention to the negative, unkind "realities" of life and pay more attention to the simple, easy expressions and demonstrations of niceness. Many years ago, someone taught me an easy method for recognizing some of the negative programming that existed in my life in just a one-week period of time, and I want to share it with you.

▣ Do the Math

On a piece of scratch paper, I want you to calculate the number of hours you spend each week with negative, garbage programming. First, calculate how many hours a week you spend reading the newspaper. I'm not referring to the funnies; I'm talking about the metro news. If it's zero hours, write a big "0."

Next, calculate how many hours per week you spend watching the news on television.

Now, how many hours a week do you spend watching soap operas, negative reality television shows, negative talk shows, or shows that degrade others?

How many hours per week do you spend watching movies with negative or violent themes? (Average the total minutes of negative or violent movies you see; for example, one two-hour movie per month equals thirty minutes per week.)

Finally, how many hours per week do you listen to or engage in gossip or negative conversation with others?

Now, total the hours you spend focusing on garbage.

Next, multiply your total garbage hours times one hundred.

Why multiply your total hours of garbage programming by one hundred? I've heard it said that for each hour you've spent focusing on negative programming or garbage, it takes a minimum of one hundred hours of positive programming to counteract the effects. If you watch a negative, violent movie for two hours, it takes two hundred hours of positive programming to undo the ill effects.

Now ask yourself, "Do I have that many hours a week to spend going to motivational seminars, reading motivational books, or listening to motivational tapes?" Of course not. So what's the answer? What do you do about it? You eliminate the negative programming. You completely divorce yourself from the garbage. You abolish it, you get rid of it, and you completely purge it from your existence. You choose *not* to watch those kinds of television shows, *not* to go to those types of violent movies, and *not* to hang around those kinds of gossipy people.

Of course, if you're as happy as you want to be, if you have all the peace of mind that you want in your life, if you have the level of self-esteem you desire and you don't want any more, then this does not apply to you. You can still gossip, go to those kinds of movies, and hang around those kinds of people to your heart's content. However, if you want to make some changes in your life and eliminate the negative programming, you may want to consider some of the following ideas that have worked well for me. And by the way, I don't know anyone who couldn't use a bit more self-esteem.

▣ Unlearn the Drama

One of the saddest things I've ever heard someone say is, "People can't change." I believe we're each born with a clean, positive slate.

Experts tell us that what children learn in the first couple of years is significant and will determine a lot about who they become as adults. Maybe Mommy and Daddy didn't teach you well, or maybe they did. But what about *now?* What are you continuing to learn? And more important, what are you deciding to *un*learn?

The following list outlines some of the many things that may be negative influences on your thinking.

The first ten minutes of a newscast: *If it bleeds, it leads.* The most negative and violent news always leads each newscast. Why? Because newscasters know they'll hook you with the drama. Isn't that a sad practice to boost viewership and ratings? The ten o'clock news will give you detailed facts about crime, violence, and bad news, but it won't tell you how many people fell in love that day. It won't tell you how many people volunteered their time that day. Since it's an ongoing, daily process to practice being nice to yourself, you need some good news.

You might be thinking, *But I have to watch the news in order to be informed.* You can become informed and be a part of world events without allowing them to depress or distract you and without buying into the unnecessary, sensationalized, negative spin on what's going on. You can become informed for one purpose: to do something about a problem or issue. You can become part of the solution rather than joining ranks with the millions of people who live in fear because they're informed of how *bad* things are. The last thing we need is more fear.

Talk shows and soap operas: Many television shows focus on gossip and negative behavior. They tend to present the most critical, tragic, and petty side of human nature. They attract an audience by bringing out the worst in people. I know people who say they turn the television on in order to have background noise while they move about their day, but don't fool yourself into thinking that that negative information doesn't get inside your head. On some level, your mind is listening, hearing, and programming the soap opera story line.

Violent themes: As a society, we've become desensitized to violence. It's commonplace in movies, videos, music, television programs, and books. This is one of the most detrimental ways to program your mind.

I was facilitating the little exercise I showed you earlier (calculating the number of hours you spend with negative, garbage programming), when a man in my audience blurted out, "Oh, please. I can watch major violent movies and they have no effect on me." Stunned, I immediately replied, "Sir, that's pretty scary. You can watch major violence, and it has no effect on you? You might want to look into that."

Have you ever watched little children as they watch violence on television? It's so unnatural to them that they squirm and take short breaths. Violence is unnatural to your physical body and loving soul—just as are bickering, critiquing, judging, and heartlessness—but many have made it part of who they are. They've hotwired their natural programming and made the unnatural and unhealthy into something natural for them. The *very* good news here is that, just as you learned to be negative, you can unlearn it.

Negative or degrading story themes: Story lines in movies, videos, music, television programs, and books that tend to be degrading to other groups of people or that have a negative premise tend to depress your thoughts and affect your emotions. Many television shows give people a platform to belittle others or send the message that people are dispensable. These shows teach that it's okay to "vote someone off the island," or proclaim someone "the weakest link." Is that what you really want going into your mind?

Gossip is not that juicy: The dictionary defines gossip as "mischievous talk about someone else's affairs." Mischievous? Is that how you'd like to be thought of and remembered? I'd like to be remembered as being fun, colorful, exciting, and entertaining, but not mischievous. And yes, you can be fun and entertaining without gossiping.

Have you ever felt the sting of someone gossiping about you? Have you noticed how unattractive others look when they gossip? Remember that your purpose is to be nice to yourself and to make yourself more attractive. Gossip does the opposite. Think long and hard about the types of conversations you engage in. And by the way, just because you're not talking the gossip, the fact that you listen to it and allow it to happen in your presence makes you a full-fledged participant, just as guilty as the person doing the talking. When you gossip, it's as though you're pointing your finger at someone and proclaiming, "They're guilty." If they're guilty, then by definition who else is guilty? You are. Remember, anytime you point your finger at someone else, three of your fingers point back at you.

If you want to eliminate negative programming, try eliminating any or all of these sources of negative drama. Start now. Control what you allow into your mind. Cut off the negative programming, the negative

TV shows, the violent movies, the gossip, and the bad news. Instead, choose to focus on that which makes your heart sing. Choose to spend time doing things that contribute to you as a person. Broaden your thought process. Focus on becoming informed, inspired, and enlightened, and discover new ways to uplift your spirits.

Step 2: Create a New Program of Things That Make You Happy

Once you've ditched the drama, you'll need to replace the negative garbage with positive programming. This can be different for every person, so you'll need to create the plan that works for you.

Take a moment to think about the things that you consider positive. What television programs could you watch? What books could you read? What audio programs could you listen to? What activities could you include into your daily life that would contribute to your well-being? Take a piece of paper and create a list of positive, uplifting things you could do to change your perspective, and then commit to that plan of conditioning.

By the way, I'm referring to *daily* conditioning. You could never go to just one motivational seminar and say, "That's it, I'm positive for life." You'd never go to just one aerobics class and say, "That's it, I'm fit for life." To create a new program of things that make you happy—things that make your heart sing—requires commitment, focus, and practice, practice, practice.

I absolutely love the connotation of the phrase "that which makes *your* heart sing." If you don't know exactly what makes your heart sing, it's fine if you just go through the motions with some of the activities suggested below until your soul catches hold.

Some people say that having fresh flowers in their house makes their day go better. If that works for you, then commit to it—nice and simple, as it should be. How about turning off the ten o'clock news and, instead, playing some soft music and lighting candles around the house? Maybe some nice conversation over dinner with a good friend is positive programming for you, or going to the gym, doing volunteer work, or reading a good book before going to bed. Here are a few more ideas to jump-start your thinking.

◻ Turn Your Car and Commuting Time into a Learning Experience

If I were asked to name one practice that would supersede all others in my personal journey to happiness, it would most definitely be listening to motivational audio programs in my car.

In 1989 I bought a new car, and thanks to the challenge given by many mentors, I decided right then and there on the showroom floor that I would never listen to music in that car. Now, I happen to love music. I have a huge CD collection and a concert grand piano in my living room. However, when I'm in my car, I consider that time to be valuable, sacred time for me. That's when I can listen to the voices of my mentors without interruption.

Even if your commute time is only ten minutes, how much better could your day be if you spent that time getting your mind focused by listening to a powerful motivational program?

◻ Drive a Clean Car

As unusual as this may seem to some people, one of the things that makes me happy is driving a clean car. My day goes so much better when I'm driving around in a clean car, yet I'll sometimes drive a dirty car for weeks. No one is going to steal my car, wash it for me, and then bring it back. My daily commitment to positive conditioning and training means doing the simple things that will make my day go better, including driving in a clean car.

◻ Watch Comedy Television Shows

Plenty of books and preachers will tell you to get rid of your television set. Although that's good advice for some, it's not for everyone. Sometimes at the end of a long day, only a mindless, silly sitcom can help me turn off my racing mind. I've read lots of motivational books, been to many positive seminars, and consider myself a nice guy, but I still own three TV sets. However, I am *very* disciplined as to what I will watch and what I won't. Trust me or ask anyone who knows me: My channel surfing won't stop on a negative or violent movie or talk show for even a second.

◻ Create a Dream Board

I'm sure that many of us would agree that our minds work more in pictures than in words. Yes, it's valuable to write things down (if you think it, ink it), but how about the *pictures* of what makes your heart sing? How about creating a *dream board?*

Either on your own, or with your family and friends, gather up as many types of magazines as you can find—fashion, architectural, travel, health, automotive, or whatever interests those in your group. For each participant, provide a large poster board, scissors, and glue. Turn on some fun or inspirational music, and maybe order in some pizza. (As you can see, I'm encouraging you to make this a fun activity, not some homework-type chore.)

Look through the magazines to discover pictures of what makes your heart sing. Perhaps it's a picture of your dream car. Maybe it's a photograph of a person who has the type of body you want. Maybe you've always wanted to take a Paris vacation, and while thumbing through a magazine, you find a photograph of the Eiffel Tower. Cut out those photos and glue them to your dream board.

Avoid judgments of what should or should not be added to your dream board. When that little voice in your head tells you, "Oh, I shouldn't want that expensive car," ignore it and listen to your heart instead. If it makes your heart sing, it belongs on your dream board. Your heart is your God-given, built-in measurement to appraise and gauge the future direction of your life—a life filled with purpose and happiness.

Once you complete your dream board, post it somewhere in your home or workspace to remind you of your new programming goals. Negative, self-doubting images can pop into your mind unannounced and uninvited, but your dream board will help you cancel them out. Make sure it's highly visible, so you're in control.

▣ Study a BE NICE Curriculum

I have a friend who, for some bizarre reason, loves reading books about serial killers. I once gave her Walt Disney's biography to read, but she said she had no interest in studying him.

It was Mac McMillan who said, "You are the same today that you'll be five years from now except for two things: the people you meet and the books you read." If you love reading trashy romance novels, then five years from now your *life* will be a trashy romance novel. But if you read inspirational stories about friendship, volunteerism, or people who've overcome amazing obstacles and accomplished incredible things, then your life will be on that path—you'll be headed toward a life that makes a difference, filled with bliss and happiness.

◨ Make a List of People in Your Life Who Are Nice

Study them. Honor them. Place their attributes of "being nice" high on your list of things to admire, celebrate, and aspire to. Place niceness over good looks, wealth, intelligence, or any other characteristic, and you'll soon begin to notice and attract nice people. That's great, because they come into your life to teach you what you most need to learn.

◨ Collect Stories of Hope and Inspiration

Look for nice, positive stories to combat the negative ones people want to share and recite. The next time someone starts telling a negative story, you can jump in with, "Yeah? But did you hear about those amazing kids who all shaved their heads so their classmate going through chemotherapy wouldn't feel out of place?"

One story that I love repeating again and again appeared in the *Boston Herald* on December 23, 1998. It's one of the nicest stories I've ever heard, and the main character was a frog-shaped lawn ornament named Phil.

In her article, "Couple Leaping for Joy over Return of Frog," Azell Murphy Cavaan described Phil and his sweetheart, Phyllis: "For eight years, the love frogs sat side-by-side on a masonry cement loveseat underneath the shade of a multicolored ceramic umbrella on Gertrude and John Knight's front lawn in Swansea. But the peace and tranquility shared by the webbed-footed duo ended abruptly when Phil was kidnapped a few days before Easter."

Soon after, postcards and letters began arriving from all over the world—from none other than Phil. The first one came from Maryland, with the message, "Sick of sitting on your front lawn. Had to get away. Love, The Frog." Others came from as far away as Zurich, London, Indonesia, and Italy—a total of thirteen postcards and twelve letters, many of which contained pictures of Phil basking in exotic locations and clearly enjoying the scenery.

Then, nine months later, just as mysteriously as he disappeared, Phil came home again—pulling up to the house in the backseat of a white, twenty-eight-foot, stretch limousine. The Knights have no idea who took their precious frog and gave them such laughter and enjoyment, and the limo driver was no help, either. It seems that the "frognapper" had not paid by credit card and had left no personal information. He simply asked the agency to pick up a "Mr. Frog" and deliver him to the

Knights. "My husband recently had lung surgery and I think he's recovering a lot faster because of this," said Gert Knight. "We just laugh and laugh every time we think about it."

Collecting and sharing stories like these can make you feel good on a regular basis. Don't wait until you're depressed or desperate to seek out positive programming and do the things I've recommended here. If you do, the most you can hope for is to dig yourself out of the hole you're in. Instead, if you program your mind and your life with positive information and experiences on a daily basis, you begin to build up a reservoir that you can draw from later. That reservoir is like a BE NICE bank account. Anytime you do get depressed, you can draw from it without feeling so spiritually and emotionally bankrupt. Depression can then be exactly what it is: a natural, normal, human emotion, not emotional bankruptcy.

Step 3: Choose Your Focus

The book *Tuesdays with Morrie* (written by Mitch Albom and published by Doubleday) had a profound effect on me about the reality we choose to focus on. The author reflected on his visits to his former professor and how those visits and the professor's impending death helped him discover a different reality. Early in the book, after his first visit with Morrie, Albom wrote about a trip to England and the colorful British tabloids:

> People scooped up these tabloids, devoured their gossip, and on previous trips to England, I had always done the same. But now, for some reason, I found myself thinking about Morrie whenever I read anything silly or mindless. I kept picturing him there, in the house with the Japanese maple and the hardwood floors, counting his breath, squeezing out every moment with his loved ones, while I spent so many hours on things that meant absolutely nothing to me personally: movie stars, supermodels, the latest noise out of Princess Di or Madonna or John F. Kennedy, Jr. In a strange way, I envied the quality of Morrie's time even as I lamented its diminishing supply. Why did we bother with all the distractions we did? Back home, the O. J. Simpson trial was in full swing, and there were people who surrendered their entire lunch hours watching it, then taped the

rest so they could watch more at night. They didn't know O. J. Simpson. They didn't know anyone involved in the case. Yet they gave up days and weeks of their lives, addicted to someone else's drama.

I remembered what Morrie said during our visit: *"The culture we have does not make people feel good about themselves. And you have to be strong enough to say if the culture doesn't work, don't buy it."*

Driving down the road of life, we all look through our windshields. We focus on where we are, what's going on around us, and where we want to go. But we also look at the rearview mirror to see where we've been and what happened back there.

Now, what's in your mind's rearview mirror? Bad drama, bad experiences, bad relationships, past mistakes, and old beliefs? Let's categorize all of that as *baggage*. You've got baggage in your rearview mirror.

If I were to ask you to share with me a name from a bad relationship you once had, I'm sure you'd be able to produce that name. That person's name and the memory of that bad relationship—that baggage—are all in your rearview mirror.

Now, here's where this gets interesting. Oftentimes we're tempted to drive down the road of life focusing *only* on the rearview mirror: "That idiot so-and-so. What he did to me . . ." If you drove down any road focusing only on your rearview mirror, what do you think would happen? You'd end up where you don't want to be, or worse—you'd probably crash. When you don't look through your windshield, and instead focus on the past and what happened "back there," you have no control over where you'll end up. You're an accident waiting to happen.

Ask yourself, *Where do I predominately choose to focus: on the road ahead or on my rearview mirror, filled with the past?* If you focus on the past, you may notice that you tend to worry about the future because your focus carries the negative experiences from your past into your present.

I'm not saying to pretend those bad things never happened. Denying them has no merit or value in your pursuit of being nice to yourself in the future. That's not what "positive mental thinking" means. I'm simply suggesting that you put your bad experiences into perspective, and just *glance* into your rearview mirror every once in a while. Maybe you're driving down the road of life toward a new relationship. Look through your windshield to the fun and excitement that lies ahead, and occasionally check out that rearview mirror for useful information: "Uh-oh, I learned that from my last relationship. I've been there before, and I'm not going to repeat that again."

You program the future—you program *tomorrow* with *today's* thoughts and beliefs. If today's beliefs include statements like "Relationships just don't work," and if today's thoughts are about how you messed things up in the past, what's tomorrow going to be like? Exactly the same, if not worse. When you continually focus and worry about how bad things were in the past, you might be destined to repeat them. *Worry* is a form of negative goal setting.

The bad experiences in your rearview mirror are meant to be valuable lessons and discoveries you've made in life, but creating a different future requires you to choose your focus carefully. Life is a choice, and how you feel about yourself today is the result of choices you made in the past.

■ ■ ■

Remember the three steps for controlling your future and you'll be well on your way to being nice to yourself: Eliminate and cancel your negative programming, create a new program of things that make you happy, and choose your focus. Go through the motions, fake it till you make it, and good self-esteem will surely follow.

Your Home-Play Assignment:

Be Selfish in a Good Way

What fills up your reservoir? What are those "good" selfish things you can do to make yourself happy in any given moment? Try this little exercise to help you find out.

Divide a sheet of paper into two columns. Label the left-hand column "Have to Do" and label the right-hand column "Nice to Do," as shown in the example below. In the left-hand column, list some things you have to do, such as "Grocery shopping" or "Taking the trash cans to the curb." In the right-hand column, come up with an activity or action that would add fun and pleasure to the "Have to Do" item. Adding "Nice to Do" activities to your "Have to Do" chores is a great way to refill your reservoir each and every day.

Have to Do	Nice to Do
Go grocery shopping	Grab a cup of java at the coffee shop across the street from the grocery store
Take the trash cans to the curb	Pet the next-door neighbor's dog after dropping the trash cans off
Mow the lawn	Put on headphones and listen to a stand-up comedian, motivational message, or favorite music while mowing
Return a long list of telephone calls	Do it while soaking in the bathtub or Jacuzzi (Just be careful not to drop the phone!)

If you're thinking, *This is so silly and simple,* then my response would be, "Thanks! It's supposed to be simple." Being nice to yourself doesn't have to be hard, so why make it difficult?

Chapter 4

Second, Boost Your Self-Esteem

"If we confine ourselves to one life role, no matter how pleasant it seems at
first, we starve emotionally and psychologically.
We need a change and balance in our daily lives.
We need sometimes to dress up and sometimes to lie around in torn jeans."
—Faye J. Crosby

The dictionary defines self-esteem as a sense of confidence and satisfaction in oneself. With that definition in mind, you might also say that self-esteem is a measure of how successful you feel. And how do you measure success? Most people answer that question by saying, "By how much money you make." It seems that many of us have been taught to believe that our value as people and our success in life are measured only by our monetary gains. Since we've been hearing that most of our lives, and since we all want to be successful, we attempt to dedicate 100 percent of our lives to our careers—only to eventually experience what's known as burnout.

It's absolutely impossible to dedicate 100 percent of your life to your career, because you're not just a "professional only" individual. Your life is divided into five basic areas. Yes, you're a professional individual, but you're also a physical, intellectual, emotional, and spiritual individual. Good self-esteem comes from the balance between all five. It's like a chain reaction: Balance is an important component for building self-esteem, self-esteem plays a vital role in your personal happiness, and happiness is necessary for cultivating niceness. Self-esteem and being nice are so closely linked that I'm dedicating this entire chapter to finding balance and building self-esteem.

The Five Areas of Balance

Before we proceed further, let me emphasize that your feelings of fulfillment in any one area are in direct proportion to the extent that you focus on achieving balance in *every* area. What does that mean? Well, if you're experiencing success with your career but you've totally ignored your spiritual needs, you won't be able to fully enjoy the financial or worthwhile benefits that your business may have produced. So why do some people spend more time designing a vacation or shopping for a pair of shoes than they spend designing a balanced life, filled with meaning and purpose? Maybe it's because focusing on having balance requires constant effort, and I'm not sure that anyone ever actually achieves it.

That thought used to depress me. I'd think, *Why can't I just coast once in a while? Why do I have to continually work on this balance thing?* But now the energy I put into designing my daily routine for feeding and nurturing all the areas of my life has become a sort of adventure—it's what gets me out of bed in the morning. Now I think, *Okay, what do I have to do today in order to end my day feeling good about myself? So I've strategized a really cool career move for today, but what's my plan for increasing my level of energy? What will I eat, what won't I eat today? So I called my mom this morning to tell her I love her, and that definitely adds purpose and balance to my life, but what can I do today to let the planet know of my heart's intentions? What charity could I get involved with, or what random act of goodness could I do for people outside my family and friends?*

The mystery of trying to figure out this balance thing can become an unfolding adventure for you, too. As you work on achieving balance in all five areas, remember that the process must be fun. That doesn't mean it will always be easy, but it must be fun. As a review from chapter 2, how do you make things fun? Two steps:

1. Find mentors and gurus for the area you want to improve.

2. Find people who want to play with and support you in your many, diverse paths of development.

Professional Balance

A lot of people hate their life from nine to five. "No pain, no gain" doesn't need to refer to your job or career. To hate something will bring to it unproductive, infertile energy. You can't "hate" your job and expect it to bring you prosperity.

I had a friend who complained about her job for years. She called me one day, very distraught, because her employers had fired her. She couldn't understand why I was so happy for her until I finally pointed out, "You hated that job and had been telling the universe about it for years. The universe finally took care of it for you. Now you have the chance to find the job you love."

How do you pursue professional balance? You ponder your balance and your plan to improve yourself professionally by remembering those two necessary steps from chapter 2. Ask yourself:

Who are my professional mentors?
Who wants to play with me professionally?

▣ My Professional Mentor

One of my business mentors happens to be a multimillionaire. I like this man a lot. But as I shared in a previous chapter, I don't believe that God gave him more potential than he gave to you or me. If my mentor can access the brilliance and potential for financial success, then that means I can do it, too—that means the "system" works.

▣ Passion Is Attractive

One of the reasons I love working with students so much is because they have what's called beginner's luck, which basically means that they don't know it won't work. I can walk into one of my schools with the stupidest idea, and my students will respond with, "Yeah, let's do it!" And guess what happens with that idea: It works! Why? Because the students have passion behind that idea, and passion is attractive.

The word *attractive* means that things will come to you, they're *attracted* to you. When you show up with passion every day, you won't have to go looking for opportunities—opportunities will come to you. You won't have to go looking for customers—they'll find you.

Occasionally, I meet someone who tells me, "Oh, I'm passionate." I want to respond with, "Then tell your face, because I can't see it right now." It's amazing how people will ready themselves for their workday by putting on their best clothes, their best shoes, do their hair and makeup—all to impress—and then walk around all day with a look of disgust, boredom, or a "boy, am I put out" type expression. Remember, it's the feeling of joy that brings you opportunities.

▣ You Play Like You Practice

In my schools, we have a philosophy that I love: YOU PLAY LIKE YOU PRACTICE. If you want to play big, you have to practice big. To play big means that you want to make more money, drive a better car, advance in your company, and be more successful in your career. To make all of that happen, you must practice big. Education is how you practice.

There are people who say they want to play big—meaning they want to earn more money—yet they don't want to practice big. A company training is announced and they whine, "Oh, do we have to go?" They want the benefits without the work. They want the results without the effort. And when they don't get the results they want, they'd rather complain than admit that there's really no mystery to why they aren't advancing.

To maintain the professional balance you need for happiness, you'll have to make an ongoing commitment to reading and studying industry-related books and magazines, as well as attending educational classes and seminars. You never want to find yourself in the position of thinking that you've "learned it all." Your career learning process will go on forever.

▣ Creative Love

A lovely woman taught me an amazing principle for creating career success. She calls it "creative love," and it's divided into three different functions and thought processes:

1. Love what you do
2. Love who you do it with
3. Love who you do it for

I know people who absolutely love what they do. They love the product or service they produce or sell, and they completely believe in its value. They also love the people they "do it for" (their customers), and they exemplify that love every single day in the way they treat them. But they're missing an important element of success because they detest their teammates—the people they "do it with." Their actions and words toward their co-workers show disdain, a lack of respect, and a complete disregard for their contribution or involvement in the company. To find professional balance, one or two of these elements is not enough. It takes all three.

Physical Balance

Having a consistent exercise program and practicing proper nutrition are both part of establishing a solid routine to maintain physical balance. If you were to approach any person who has a daily or weekly routine for maintaining physical balance, and ask whether giving up that routine would somehow have a negative effect on the person's career or relationships, the answer would be, "Most definitely." A consistent commitment to physical balance will help you acquire balance in the other areas of your life. Your relationships, your performance at work, and your own self-esteem will dramatically improve.

Please note that we're talking about balance, not excess. Unless bodybuilding is part of your career, then more than a sufficient number of hours per week working out in a gym might not translate into all-around balance. And don't just begin and end your physical balance routine with an exercise regime. Perhaps you need more sleep at night, more rest. How about devoting quiet time for meditation, yoga, or relaxation? Perhaps you need to take care of yourself physically by making an appointment with a doctor or dentist. Perhaps a weekly massage would do the trick, or eating a balanced and healthy diet. Maybe it's as simple as supplementing your diet with vitamins, or incorporating homeopathic remedies or Chinese herbs.

Once again, please ponder your physical balance and your plan to improve yourself physically by asking:

Who are my physical mentors?
Who wants to play with me to keep balance physically?

◫ Choosing Physical Mentors

When choosing physical mentors, would you want to go to the gym with someone in better shape or worse shape than you? The answer is *BETTER!* Why? Because people who are already ahead of you make the best mentors. If they did it, then you can, too.

▣ Finding People to Play With

As for finding people who want to support you and play with you while moving toward physical balance, I consider myself an expert on this subject. I go to the gym at least four or five days per week, but I don't naturally enjoy going. Now, just because I don't enjoy something, does that mean I have the option to not do it? No. So what options do I have? To make it fun. And how do I make it fun? Well, first I figured out what "fun" means *to me*. I happen to love being around people—that's my idea of the most fun I can possibly have—so I get as many people to go to the gym with me as possible.

I have a pool of about five or six friends whom I can recruit to exercise with on a regular basis, and usually there are at least three of us in the gym together each time we go. We're dedicated to the process and focused about why we're there, but none of us is entering physique competitions. We go together for the balance, the fun, the conversations, the camaraderie, the escape, and more. I don't think I could ever stay focused or committed in a home gym. I need the ritual of going to a place where there are many people, all there for the same purpose, with the motivating music, the clanging of weights, and the loud coaching of an aerobics or spinning instructor in the adjacent room. I think of the gym as sort of a temple, and I've set myself up to beat the "I'm too busy" or "I'm too tired" routine. I make sure that I have friends who keep me on track on those days when I'm pooping out, and I do the same for them on their off days.

I remember once after an exercise-recruiting session in one of my schools ("Wanna go? Wanna go?"), two of my students and one of my instructors all said, "Yeah, we wanna go." So we went. The two students and I were lifting weights in one part of the gym, while our other companion, a sixty-year-old woman who happened to have a new pink leotard, ran conspicuously around the gym, obviously trying to get a laugh out of us. She'd hang upside down, facing the wrong way on the machines, while the fitness instructors whispered to each other, "What's that big pink woman doing over there?" The three of us were laughing hysterically at our school instructor, but what happened? We had a great workout, and it was fun. All because we practiced those two simple rules: We found physical mentors to keep us on track, and we found people who wanted to play together.

───────────── ▣ ─────────────

Intellectual Balance

If you ask children what makes them happy, they can go on and on. Ask some average adults what makes them happy, and many respond with, "Hmmm, that's a tough one. But I could tell you what upsets me." We sometimes have a strong connection to what doesn't work in our lives, but not much of a connection to what does work. This often leads to a sense of burnout.

Contrary to popular opinion, burnout doesn't always have to do with working too much. I know people who lie on the couch all day, and they're burned out. Why? Because they lack intellectual balance.

Intellectual balance has to do with stimulating your mind in ways other than those required by your career. For example, you might develop your intellectual balance by trying scuba diving lessons, learning a second language, taking singing lessons, or learning how to work a personal computer. You could take a night class in art history at a local college, a pottery class as a way to relax your mind and body, or try something brand-new you've never tried before. Your intellectual stimulation could come from books, audiotapes, workshops, or intelligent dinner conversation with a good friend. Maybe you'd like to make a pact with your spouse and friends to not "talk shop" after hours, and instead explore topics other than work.

The formula for developing intellectual balance is the same as for all the other areas. Make it fun by asking yourself:

Who are my intellectual mentors?
Who wants to play with me intellectually?

▣ Make It a Habit

No matter what interests you, gets your mind going, and makes your heart sing, it's a good idea to set up some type of routine for focusing on intellectual balance. I personally spend a great deal of time in my car and have devoted all of my driving time to listening only to motivational and educational audiotapes and CDs. Now, you might think it's quite extreme to not listen to music. I love music. In fact, I'm a musician myself and have played the piano since I was fourteen years old. However, I devote all of my driving time to listening to what is now a very large collection of motivational audiotapes and CDs. I'm in my fifth car since I started this good habit—I figure that's enough listening time to have a college degree by now.

Some people find that fifteen minutes of reading a good book (not a trashy novel or a murder-mystery suspense thriller) right before bedtime fills their intellectual need. I've heard it said that the mind is most aware and impressionable during the first waking hours. If that were true, you'd be wise to feed your mind with nothing but powerful, motivating, or stimulating information first thing in the morning. Maybe a motivational tape or CD playing in the bathroom while you get dressed in the morning could fit the bill.

◪ Why Bother?

At a dinner party in my home once, a friend looked at my piano and told me that ever since he was a young child, he'd always wanted to take piano lessons. When I told him that I knew of a really good piano teacher in town, and that I'd love to hook him up, he responded, "I'm an adult now. Why bother?"

A curious mind is attractive, and attractive people bring to themselves adventures for growth and new experiences. I believe that low self-esteem is tied to boredom, while high self-esteem is exactly the opposite. When people are continuously interested in new things, that trait releases within them a natural high.

◪ Do What You Love

Remember the term *hobby?* A hobby is something you love to do. You may not be good at it, and you may never make money at it, but it's something that makes your heart sing.

Perhaps you just *love* cooking, but no one will touch your food. That's okay. You cook anyway, because it makes your heart sing.

Hobbies can bring purpose and passion back to your daily life. Look at it this way: Your mind leads you toward logical things, but maybe it's your heart that leads you toward hobbies, and hobbies create passion and purpose. Learn to surrender and follow your heart.

Emotional Balance

Emotional balance has to do with relationships. First and foremost is the relationship you have with yourself—you must master that relationship before you can work on your relationship with others. Hence the importance of the message and practices in the last chapter: First, be nice to yourself.

As for relationships with others, oftentimes people think that relationships have only to do with that "one and only" intimate, special person in their life. However, emotional balance goes beyond that. Every person you come in contact with is a relationship that requires your commitment. To improve emotional balance and strengthen all of your relationships, ask yourself once again:

Who are my emotional mentors?
Who wants to play with me emotionally?

▣ Every Contact Is a Relationship

Do you ever drive in traffic? If so, you have a relationship with everyone on the freeway. How you choose to conduct yourself in that traffic situation will determine the amount of personal balance you'll have in your life. If you drive down the freeway screaming, "Get out of my way!" it's going to be very difficult for you to walk into work and say, "Hi, happy to serve you." If you verbally abuse waiters, waitresses, or bank tellers, it's going to be very difficult for you to have a successful, intimate relationship with a spouse or partner.

Every person you come in contact with is a relationship and therefore an opportunity for you to grow, learn, and balance yourself emotionally. If you just assume that everyone is doing the best that they know how to do—just as you are—and choose to give people a break, you'll find yourself achieving the emotional balance you desire.

▣ Love Everyone, but Put Yourself First

It's amazing the rollercoaster ride some people choose to put themselves through in the dating and romance scene. When the gurus, poets, and masters talk about "loving everyone," that doesn't mean you have to give your phone number to everyone. It doesn't mean you have to always spend time and hang out with everyone. Sometimes to maintain your emotional balance, you must first love yourself enough to stay away from people who aren't nice to you, or who make you feel less of yourself. You aren't staying away as an "attack" on them; you're staying away because you love yourself enough to stay away.

◙ Long-Lasting Loves

How much do you invest in your friendships? I was never the type of person to get a new set of friends each year, and I've always prided myself on my long-term friendships. My two best friends are Dennis and Dianne, and we've been in each other's lives forever. I love telling people that I've had knock-down, drag-out fights (not literally) with each of my two best friends, and that they've made us that much more trusting and loving of each other. Some amazing depth is added to friendships when you can see each other in the worst light and still choose to love and be loyal to each other.

◙ My Relationship Mentors

I mentioned this in an earlier chapter, but it bears repeating in this section on relationship mentors. I am fortunate in the fact that my parents have been happily and romantically married for sixty years. When I spend time with them, I see that they're just as romantic with each other now as they've been for as long as I can remember. Ten times a day I catch them hugging, kissing, and saying to each other, "Oh, I love you so much."

My father's getting up there in age, and some health issues have slowed him down a bit, yet he still won't let my mother lift a finger. He wants to wait on her hand and foot. Whenever she wants or needs something, my father jumps up and tells her, "Jeanne, I'll get it. I'll get it!" When he does that, my mother giggles as if she were a sixteen-year-old schoolgirl all over again. She just blossoms when he treats her that way.

My parents laugh about the fact that their bodies are falling apart, and they think it's funny that they forget everything. Yes, they're my relationship mentors. I think to myself, *If they can maintain romance for sixty years, then there's hope for me.*

Spiritual Balance

Spiritual balance is often described only in conjunction with religious beliefs. However, in this section I wish to propose that spiritual balance means *having peace of mind with what you believe in.* I know a lot of very religious people who go to their church, temple, or mosque every week, but some of them don't seem to have peace of mind with what they believe in. In fact, sometimes, rather than bringing them peace of mind, their beliefs bring them more guilt, fear, and judgment of others—they bring out the worst in them. To me, that's not spirituality.

As you ponder this idea of spiritual balance and work on developing your plan to improve yourself spiritually, remember to ask yourself:

Who are my spiritual mentors?
Who wants to play with me spiritually?

As you go seeking your spiritual mentors and playmates, I'd like to respectfully offer some take-it-or-leave-it advice: Those you seek may come from unexpected places.

I used to discard valuable information simply because it didn't come from a priest, pastor, or prophet. But I learned not to judge the source of information and wisdom that works for me. In other words, if I hear something that has value and meaning to help me become a better person, the source doesn't matter.

▣ Finding Spiritual Mentors

Not that I've often admitted this, but I know what I'm capable of—in a *negative* way. If I were to allow myself, I know how low I could go. Therefore, I do all that I can to keep myself on track. I need spiritual mentors, tutors, guides, teachers, and gurus. I need *all* of them. And they come from every walk of life, religion, color of people, and social scale.

In addition to the obvious spiritual mentors and comrades, try looking in other places. In fact, look *everywhere*. Maybe your best mentors and spiritual allies never step foot in a church or synagogue. Your spiritual guru could be sitting on the surfboard next to you waiting for the next wave. Your spiritual ally could be the tattooed, multipierced convenience store cashier. Your spiritual guide could be the kindergarten-age child who seems to do nothing but smile and stare at you on an airplane. Wow! Think of the possibilities.

Years ago, after driving my cherished BMW convertible for over 120,000 miles, I was on my way home from leading a very lucrative motivational seminar when my dream car decided to blow up on the freeway. Luckily, I was able to coast off an exit and right into the parking lot of a nearby convenience store.

Once I gathered my thoughts and threw a "poor me" pity party, I realized I was in an unsafe part of town. I also realized I wasn't alone.

Although I hadn't immediately noticed him, I soon became aware of a man who had instantly run to my aid. Apparently, he'd seen my car coast into the parking lot and, for some reason, decided to take me on as his project and to protect me. While I angrily used my cell phone to call a tow truck, he proceeded to comfort me by telling me that he was an auto mechanic. He quickly began working under my smoking raised hood, all the while conversing with me in what I remember to be a very kind, comforting conversation. "Where are you from? What do you do?" he asked. "I hope your family isn't worried about you. I'll try to find out what the problem is and see if I can fix your car."

After being told by the tow truck company that it would be more than an hour's delay, and after my stranger-mechanic friend reluctantly proclaimed no hope for my BMW, I halfway surrendered to what I'd previously considered to be an annoying conversation. I began to answer his questions about who I was, adding, "No, my family won't be worried about me. Thanks for asking." I then told him that I was a motivational speaker on my way home from a seminar I'd just facilitated in Los Angeles.

"Oh, you mean like Zig Ziglar?" he asked.

"Yes," I proclaimed.

"I used to listen to Zig Ziglar tapes. I loved those tapes."

"Well, I've got some motivational tapes of my own in the trunk," I said, as I opened the trunk and offered him, *for free*, a set of my motivational tapes. My newfound friend continued on with his kind conversation and words of consolation for my unfortunate situation, and assured me that he would stay with me until the tow truck arrived.

After listening to his relentless comforting for a while, I finally started asking my rescuer about himself. "What's your name?" I asked.

"Brian," he answered.

"What do you do?"

"I've worked as an auto mechanic."

"Where do you live?"

"Over there," he pointed.

"In that apartment building behind the convenience store?"

"No," he replied.

"Where then?" I asked.

"In my car, with my wife and my little boy, behind the store."

With a huge flood of emotion, I suddenly realized what a fool I'd been. For over two hours, this kind, unassuming man had comforted, humored, and protected this high-priced, BMW-driving, motivational "expert." And although I offered him money, and a "let's go to the grocery store" proposal, the only thing he would take from me—gratefully and humbly—was my motivational tape series. And oh, how grateful he was. "I'll cherish this forever!" he proclaimed as I climbed into the cab of the tow truck.

Right then and there, I felt as if the entire universe was grinning at me with a sort of "Silly boy" type response. Oh, did I have a lot to learn about where my next teacher would come from and who knows what else.

A lot of preachers and motivational speakers (including me) claim to be many things, but this man was the true guru for those two hours. If I'd had a tape recorder or a camera with me that day, the masses would have been impressed by his example.

▣ Find Your Own Path

The routines for acquiring spiritual balance are different for each individual. For some, spending weekends at the beach or up in the mountains, where they can clear their mind and take in nature, helps them balance themselves spiritually. For others, doing volunteer work brings peace of mind.

Perhaps devoting time to a favorite charity could help you step outside your own drama, do something good for someone else, and help you acquire spiritual balance. Learning how to be more grateful, and showing your gratitude often to many people, can bring a centeredness and calmness to your being, which brings about peace of mind and spirituality.

For me, my sense of spirituality has a direct relationship with the good I do in the world. And when I say *good*, I'm not just referring to volunteerism. Although there are many causes and charities that tug at my heartstrings, I'm never able to devote the amount of time to those charities that I would like. I used to think, *Oh, I'll feed the hungry two weeks from Thursday, from five till seven.* Yeah, right. That rarely happened, and as long as my sense of purpose and spirituality was linked to the number of hours I devoted to volunteerism, I never felt spiritual.

Here's how I changed both my thinking and my actions: I realized that I can do "volunteer work" all day, every day. What do I mean by that? Let me give you some examples.

I'm not required to smile at every person I meet; I'm not paid to do that. So if I choose to do it, it's on a *volunteer* basis and therefore I'm giving something that I'm not required to give—and that makes me feel good about myself. I'm not required to notice and hug the student in my school who's experiencing loneliness or some type of struggle, so if I do hug that student, it's on a *volunteer* basis. It's that simple.

As for raising money, I don't always have to wait for a charitable fundraising event. As a business owner, I can offer the products and services of my business to support, serve, and give back to people in my community on a daily basis. On a typical day, if a hundred clients come in, perhaps two of them will receive something extra, or they won't pay at all. I can *volunteer* to make those kinds of decisions, so why not?

If you're not a business owner, that doesn't mean you can't use your place of employment as a vehicle to make a difference in your community. Making a difference isn't always about donating time or money to a cause. If you're a waiter or waitress, your smiles, kind words, and calling total strangers "darling" can make a difference and heal someone in need, whether you realize it or not. I can count numerous times when a waitress was my "angel of mercy," so to speak, on a particular day when I needed a little boost. If you're a grocery bagger or checkout clerk, you have the opportunity every single day to tell hundreds of people to have a good day, and to truly mean it.

Bestselling author and lecturer Marianne Williamson used to say that every business is a front for a church, but I don't think she was referring to a place of worship or a religion. What I translated that to mean for me is that every business—whether it be a pizza parlor, an accounting firm, a hospital, or a beauty salon—can be a place where both customers and employees feel accepted, loved, cared for, and safe.

People in need are not just those who line up at a soup kitchen. There are people all around you who suffer spiritually, mentally, emotionally, healthwise, financially, and in so many other ways. They could be people you work with every day, and you just don't know it. They could be members of your own family, your neighbors, or people in your religious congregation.

It's so worthwhile to note that the spiritual gifts you offer are not only for the benefit of the receiver. You can be generous and giving out of your own self-interests. Your own spirit and soul need continual nourishing, and you do that by giving of yourself. As Shirley Chisholm, the first African American woman elected to Congress, said, "Service is the rent you pay for room on this earth."

Putting It All Together

You know those nights when you go to bed, and even though you're physically exhausted, your mind won't let you sleep? Your head hits the pillow and all of a sudden your eyes are wide open and your mind is going a hundred miles per hour. Do you know why that is? It may be because you don't have balance in all five areas of your life.

Perhaps you know that you don't practice proper nutrition, so your mind is racing, trying to find that balance for you. Or you know that you don't cultivate healthy, constructive relationships, so again your mind is racing, trying to find that balance.

Do you know anyone who's perfectly balanced in all five areas? To tell you the truth, I can't think of anyone who's achieved that perfect balance. Usually, the routine is that you spend a lot of time at work trying to get balanced with your career, and all of a sudden you realize you've got a pot belly. So then you spend time at the gym trying to achieve balance physically, but your spouse starts complaining that you're never home. So then you spend time at home trying to get balanced emotionally, in your relationships, and before you realize it, you haven't done volunteer work in awhile. So you spend time doing volunteer work to get that spiritual balance, and before you know it, you realize you're not making enough money. So there you are back at work again, trying to achieve balance with your career.

The excitement in life comes from trying to achieve balance. Recognize that all five areas exist and remember that you can't put any area of your life on hold. You can't say to yourself, "I'm not going to be a spiritual person for the next three years while I get my career off the ground." You can't do that because, again, if you focus too much on any one area, you'll experience burnout and (as Louise Hay describes it) dis-ease.

🔲 🔲 🔲

Above all else, please remember:

Balance = Self-Esteem = Happiness = Niceness

Your Home-Play Assignment:

Balancing All Five Areas

One last time, if you haven't done so already, please consider the five areas of life and ask yourself the two key questions for each:

Who are my professional mentors?
Who wants to play with me professionally?

Who are my physical mentors?
Who wants to play with me to keep balance physically?

Who are my intellectual mentors?
Who wants to play with me intellectually?

Who are my emotional mentors?
Who wants to play with me emotionally?

Who are my spiritual mentors?
Who wants to play with me spiritually?

Chapter 5

What Happens When You Blow It?
(And You Will!)

"Fall seven times, stand up eight."
—Japanese proverb

I f you're like most people, you probably consider yourself to be nice most of the time. Then all of a sudden, you find yourself in a situation where an unimaginable monster comes out of you. Perhaps being around screaming children turns you into a beast, or sitting in rush-hour traffic transforms you into a demon your own family would be shocked to witness.

Let's face it. You're going to blow this BE NICE thing. You're going to blow it a lot. Why? Welcome to the human race. There's no such thing as consistency in your thoughts, moods, behaviors, actions, personality, or character. Everything is in a cycle. The seasons change. The tide comes in, and then it goes out. Your nice factor is strong on some days, and on other days a million dollars couldn't keep you on track.

Yes, you'll blow it. You'll preach and practice being nice, and then turn around and do the exact opposite.

What Causes You Not to Be Nice?

Which circumstances chase being nice right out the window for you? Pay attention and watch for the signals, because everyone has them. In fact, you might want to ask your family and close friends to lovingly point out the "buttons" that cause your niceness to dissipate. Is it when you have to wait in a slow-moving line? When your nagging mother calls? When you're around screaming babies? In a crowded airport? Dealing with a rude waiter?

If only they were different and would change first,
then I could be nice.

For me, it's usually when I'm tired that I'm not nice. When I'm tired, I get cranky, I become abrupt with people, and I act unkindly. I know that about myself, so I acknowledge it and share it with others. I will say, however, that on those occasions when I blow it and I'm not nice, I realize it within hours or even minutes. Years ago, it took me days, weeks, months, and maybe even years before I realized where and when I'd blown it, gotten off track, hadn't been nice, screwed up a relationship, and therefore screwed up my own happiness and peace of mind. Now, because I have the awareness and presence of mind to realize that it's *not* because other people are extra irritating in that moment, but that the issue lies with me, I usually have the good sense to force a smile and let them know I'm tired. That's it. I'm done.

Yes, you're going to blow it and make some mistakes along your path. Making the mistake is one thing, but beating yourself up over it can become your second mistake. If you can identify the patterns or circumstances that cause you to be mean, and take responsibility for your own actions, you're one step closer to being nice. Meanwhile, let's look at some methods of damage control for those occasions when you aren't so nice.

How to Fix It When You've Blown It

What do you do when you realize you've blown it? Here are three different options. Choose the one you like the best:

1. **Justify your meanness.** Tell yourself that the person you weren't nice to somehow deserved it: *"They had it coming because they aren't nice."*

2. **Apologize, but make an excuse and place blame for why you weren't nice.** Offer any or all of the following excuses: *"I'm having a really bad day. I didn't get enough sleep last night.*

That's just my personality. My boss is in a really bad mood today. My best friend was a jerk to me. I have a toothache. This damn economy has me on edge."

3. **Sincerely apologize.** No excuse. No blame. No explanation. No guilt: *"You know what? What I just did or said wasn't very nice, and I sincerely apologize. Can we start all over?"*

Okay, that was a trick question. The first two choices won't make you a nice person. The correct answer is number three: Sincerely apologize when you blow it. (But you already knew that, didn't you?)

Even Nice People Have an "Off" Day

At times, even though you really are a nice person, you'll have an off day or be mean in a difficult situation. When that happens, it's easy to pass judgment on yourself and decide you're not nice. Instead, don't be so quick to judge. Give yourself a break. Assume you're doing the best you know how in that moment. Ask yourself, "Has the nicest person I know ever been a jerk?" If you think the answer is no, then you obviously didn't understand the question.

Come on, admit it. We all act like jerks on occasion, behaving very differently from our usual personality. For whatever reason, we do the opposite of our true character. Since we know that's true, let's assume we're doing the best we know how—and sometimes we simply have an off day.

If Einstein had had an unintelligent day, do you think people would've said, "Oh, I met him once, and he said something stupid, so he really wasn't that intelligent"? If they saw Arnold Schwarzenegger devouring a fat-filled buffet, would they say, "Oh, he's really not into fitness"? Of course not. Yet if someone has one "bad" encounter with someone who's usually nice 364 days a year, they'll forever tell their friends that the person was a jerk.

Suppose you had a chance meeting with a famous celebrity, say in a restaurant, and because your thirty-second encounter with that celebrity was not a joyous meeting, filled with conversation and hugging, you decided she wasn't nice. You tell your friends, "Yeah, I met that movie star, and she was a real bitch!" Think about it. That celebrity could be the most loving mother to her children, an amazing wife, a giving volunteer, and respectful to all her colleagues, but she's now branded as a bitch by someone who shouldn't have an opinion. We do this to celebrities, we do this to people we know, and we do it to ourselves. Instead of branding people "not nice" because of one encounter or behavior, let's try to remember that even nice people have an off day.

Choose a Better Yardstick

Why would you invest your time and energy in believing that someone is mean or nasty? Is it so you can justify your own shortcomings, and therefore become a lazy couch potato instead of fine-tuning your own nice factor?

I remember this guy telling me why he watched negative gossipy television shows: He figured that since his own life wasn't as disgusting as the guests portrayed on those shows, he must not be doing too badly. In other words, he used another person's miserable existence as a yardstick to measure his own happiness. That's one of the silliest things I've ever heard.

Just as you wouldn't want to measure your health and wellness by comparing yourself to an unhealthy, overweight, lazy, chain-smoking, junk-food addict, it's important to avoid the easy trap of comparing yourself to mean Neanderthals.

Beware the Traps You Set

Have you ever been in the presence of someone and just waited for them to screw up? Did you notice that, sooner or later, they did screw up? It would have been difficult for them not to. When you set traps for people, they sometimes fall right into them. It's like driving a car with someone and constantly telling them what a bad driver they are. What happens? They become one. They might normally be a careful, courteous driver, but because you think they're a maniac driver, they start driving like a maniac.

If you assume that people are mean and nasty, they'll be a bit more mean and nasty than normal. If you assume that people are nice, thoughtful, loving, and doing the best they know how in that moment, then they're free to become those wonderful things. Your belief in their niceness gives them permission to move in the direction of being a better person. It's called a gift. Believing that people are good, decent, and nice is a gift you give them, and they can now be nicer than they've ever been before.

If you thought this chapter was only about keeping other people from blowing it, think again. As *A Course in Miracles* teaches, a thought does not escape its source. What you think about other people, you think about yourself. What you deny other people, you deny yourself. But it's also true that when you choose to give gifts to others—gifts of compassion and forgiveness—you begin to give those same gifts to yourself.

Definition of a Gift

Have you ever opened the door at a store or restaurant for a total stranger, who then walked right through without saying, "Thanks"? Didn't you just want to run up and trip them? For many people, ungrateful behavior causes them to blow this BE NICE thing.

Here's how to look at it instead. If you open the door for a total stranger, that's a gift you've given them. True? Well, you can have no preconceived ideas or opinions as to what people do with your gifts. In other words, if you're standing there waiting for that person to say "Thank you," is that a gift? No. That would be like me buying you a shirt for your birthday, and then if you didn't wear it the next day, I became mad and upset. Is that a gift? No, it's a contract. One of my all-time favorite mentors, Marianne Williamson, said that in the 1960s she'd get really angry with people who wouldn't sign her peace treaty. Think about it.

Believe me, there will be plenty of times when you'll give the gift of being nice to people and they may not notice or accept it. They may even react negatively, asking, "Why are you so annoyingly nice all the time?" Instead of letting their reaction cause you to blow it, just remember that you gave the gift. Giving gifts *always* makes you feel better about yourself, and isn't that what this whole book is about?

Who's Your Bitch-Buddy?

Have you ever had one of those days when you just didn't feel like being nice? Do you ever feel like this BE NICE thing is just a bunch of crap? Well, let me say once again, welcome to the human race. Of course you'll have days when you don't feel like being nice. Everyone does. We all need time to process, whine, moan, and complain. It's a natural part of who we are. What's important, however, is that when you're having one of those days, you don't pollute everyone around you. Instead, you need a "bitch-buddy."

My friends and co-workers have used and practiced this system for many years. In fact, we're quite up-front about it. We call it our "Who's Your Bitch-Buddy?" system.

A bitch-buddy is someone you can gripe to—a nonjudgmental, confidential sounding board. A bitch-buddy is a person you can talk to when you feel bitter, mean, nasty, and ugly.

I've known my bitch-buddy, Dennis, since we were young children, and he's been my best friend for many, many years. Dennis has also worked with me in my company for sixteen years, and he's the one person I go to when I need to vent. At least once a week, I let Dennis know that I need a "session" with him—I need for him to be my listening, nonjudgmental ear as I download my latest thoughts, adventures, and struggles.

I've learned through past mistakes that if I were to whine and complain to friends or team members who perhaps didn't understand that I was just having an off day, they'd jump to all sorts of inaccurate conclusions: *Uh-oh, Winn's depressed. I'd better warn everyone. The company must be in trouble. My paycheck is going to bounce. I'd better find a new job.*

You might be thinking, *Winn, why do you need a bitch-buddy so often?* Please know that I'm not always whining and complaining in my sessions with Dennis. Most of the time, I just need a sounding board—I just need to hear my own voice speak my own thoughts. I don't want to gamble with the words I speak, so my bitch-buddy fits the bill.

I don't know about you, but my mind races with all sorts of ideas and feelings. Some I wish to claim, some I don't. Some of my thoughts and feelings are as foreign to me as one of those crazy dreams we all have on occasion, when we wake up and think, *Where did that come from?* Mix those foreign thoughts and feelings with day-to-day struggles and challenges, and before you know it, I'm wondering, *Where's Dennis?* Bottom line, my sessions with Dennis are more about my growth than they are about negative complaining and drama.

Bitch-Buddy Guidelines

Here are some guidelines to help you partner with your bitch-buddy in the most productive and effective ways.

First, decide who your bitch-buddy could be. Choose wisely, because the role that this person plays in your life is as important as having a great therapist, coach, medical doctor, or financial advisor. Perhaps sharing this book with some of your friends and confidants, and then asking for their input and response, could help you find out who your bitch-buddy might be. Once you know, then the two of you "contract" with each other.

You and your bitch-buddy agree that:

- You only get *one* bitch-buddy to bitch to. If you make it a bad habit of bitching to more than one person, eventually half don't want to hear it and the other half think you deserve your problems.

- Your bitch-buddy isn't just for bitching. You must also share the news when things are going great.

- The bitch-buddy system goes both ways: You take turns and each be a buddy to the other.

Temper, Temper, Temper

Yeah, I have one. Don't you? Don't most people? Years ago, that temper—that alien monster who lives inside me and chooses to make appearances at very inopportune moments in my life—would take over my heart, mind, and soul about 30 percent of the time. I can honestly say that I've gotten that monster to limit its visits to maybe only 5 percent of the time, and my focus is to get it down to even less than that. But I can't deny that I have a temper.

Now, how did I go from 30 percent of the time down to only 5 percent? I did exactly what I've been sharing in this book. I smile at total strangers. I send love notes to my friends. I call my mother almost every day. I go to the gym. I do volunteer work. I eat a good breakfast. I hug my staff and customers at work. Need I go on?

Quit thinking there's some secret pill that will turn you into a nice person. It takes work, but the work is not a mystery. How will I limit

BITCH-BUDDY CONTRACT

How to Be a Bitch-Buddy

1. You must sit and LISTEN. Only give advice and input if they are requested.

2. You absolutely cannot use the information outside of the conversation in which it was shared. You cannot share it with other people, and you cannot bring it up with the person at another time.

3. The next day, the person who bitched to you will most likely be back to their wonderful, positive self. You cannot bring up the bitch session or information that was shared with you the previous day.

The bitch-buddy system works best when one person is bitching and one is supporting. The bitch session is not for matching wits, comparing stories, or having a who-had-the-worst-day competition.

My Bitch-Buddy Promise

- YES, I will be your bitch-buddy.
- You can complain, moan, whine, and bitch to me on those days when you need to get mean, nasty, and ugly.
- I promise not to judge or think less of you, because you need to express yourself.
- I promise that I will not do anything with the information you share.
- I promise that I will not repeat it to *anyone*.
- I promise that I will not give you advice or feedback unless you ask me to.
- I promise that I will not hold the information against you later.
- When you request a bitching session, I promise to hold back my personal complaints and woes for another bitching session at another time.

Signed _____

my temper to less than it is now? I'll continue doing exactly what I'm sharing in this book.

Pay It Forward

Sometimes you're not nice and, for whatever reason, you can't go back and apologize to people for having been mean, malicious, or unkind to them. The main thing to realize is that feeling guilty will only delay and obstruct the lessons and practices of becoming a nicer person. It seems and feels better to recognize that you blew it and vow to make it right for the next person you come into contact with by "paying it forward."

In her wonderful book, *Pay It Forward*, Catherine Ryan Hyde wrote that even though you can't always pay back the people who have helped you along the way, you can "pay it forward" to someone else. You can build up a spiritual and "good karma" bank account, so to speak, so the help and kindness continue to flow.

In a similar way, you can pay it forward as a way to make up for the apologies you weren't able to deliver to the people you've wronged. If your bad experiences with addiction, divorce, abuse, or whatever caused you to not be nice in the past, but have since helped you to open your mind, soften your heart, and let go of judgments and prejudices, then good for you. Perhaps you won't be able to use your new life skills with the people you wronged while going through those experiences, but you'll be able to use them with future relationships. I'd like to tell you a story about what can happen when you pay it forward.

Years ago, I went to dinner with a good friend of mine who, like some people, has a tendency to feel down a lot of the time. He was telling me about a seminar he'd attended, where the speaker had said that if you want to be happy, just silently in your mind send this message to every person you come in contact with: "I love you." My friend left the seminar thinking, *Well, that was pretty stupid. I came to this seminar to get some good advice, and all they told me was to walk around silently telling people that I love them.*

A couple of days after the seminar, he was at the bank. Standing in line, he noticed that the bank teller was being quite harsh and abusive toward every customer she served. She was practically biting people's heads off. As he watched this go on with one person after another, he suddenly realized, *My gosh, I'm next!* As he waited in line, getting closer and closer, he thought he might as well try what the speaker had taught. Just as he was about to approach the teller's window, he looked at her and silently said to her in his mind, *I love you.*

As he stepped up to her window, she looked up and it was as if she was a different person. She was totally transformed. She looked at my friend, smiled her first smile, and as she asked, "May I help you?" he just stood there with a blank surprised look on his face. After he left the bank, he just flew through the rest of the day. He couldn't believe that the simple gesture of sending an unspoken thought could have such a major impact on his *own* self-esteem.

Upon hearing this story, Vivienne, a dear friend of mine, shared with me that she'd be willing to experiment with this magic energy of silently saying *I love you* to family and friends, but not to total strangers. With them, she might require more discernment in order to be conscious of what she might project and attract. Vivienne recommends that if silently saying "I love you" is too challenging when you meet someone new, you might instead embrace the silent statement, *You are important.*

The moral of all of this is, you only get what you give in life. If you're feeling a lack of love in your life, go out and give love to other people. If you're feeling like people don't understand you, try to understand them first. If you're feeling a lack of support, give all your support to other people. And if you're feeling that people aren't nice, try being nice to them first.

We've been kind of a spoiled generation, haven't we? We make statements like "I'm waiting for my ship to come in." Let me ask you, how many ships have you sent out lately? The only things lacking in your life right now are the things you aren't giving, the things you're holding onto. You know, you need three hugs a day just to keep from being weird. You might be thinking, *Oh my gosh, Winn, that's why I'm so weird—because I don't get three hugs a day.* You know why you don't get three hugs a day? Because you don't deserve them. You don't deserve them because you don't give them. You only get what you give in life.

I know people who, the minute they feel a little sniffle in their nose, immediately begin to load up on vitamin C as a quick, easy way to heal and prevent a looming cold. What if you did the same thing to avoid a looming attack of blowing your nice factor? When you feel like you're about to blow it, try incorporating some of the quick, easy solutions from this chapter to both prevent and heal the times when you blow it.

Your Home-Play Assignment:

Pay It Forward

The next time you feel a little down, depressed, or unappreciated, I challenge you to try something like what my friend did. Go to the mall, walk from one end to the other, and as you pass each person, just look them in the eye and silently say to them, "I wish you happiness. I wish you peace of mind. I wish you happiness." If, by the time you get to the other end of the mall, you're not feeling better about yourself, turn around, go back the other way, and do it again. By offering this gift to total strangers, you pay it forward and undo the acts of meanness you displayed toward others.

Does this sound hokey? Does it sound contrived? You bet it does. And yet it works. Is this the end-all solution to your problems? Probably not, but it certainly puts you in a better frame of mind to deal with the things you're working on.

Being Nice at Home

*"A man travels the world over in search of what he needs
and returns home to find it."*
—George Moore

Your home life growing up is where you learn how to *be* in the
world. After you leave home to live in the world, you sometimes need to return home to practice what you've learned and
to heal relationships with family members. When you heal and grow
those family relationships, you're better equipped, more mature, and
ready to go back into the world to be someone new and improved. As
that new and improved person, you gain confidence and insight. You
then return back home to use the skills you've learned in the world and
cultivate an even better home life. That's the process—going from
home to the world and back home again, all part of the process of
becoming whole.

Whether you're forty, sixty, or eighty years old, you never outgrow
the fact that you have a father, a mother, grandparents, perhaps some
siblings, maybe some aunts, uncles, and cousins. Learning to become
your true, adult, lovely self comes from granting significance to all
those relationships—it comes from *being nice at home*. Let's call being
nice at home a "homecoming," both metaphorically and literally.
That's what this chapter is all about.

A Season, a Reason, a Lifetime

A good friend once shared with me the idea that people enter your life for a season, a reason, or a lifetime. As I look back over all the relationships I've had with anyone and everyone, each could be placed into one of those categories—season, reason, or lifetime relationships.

A "season relationship" could happen with a new friend you meet on vacation. You have a wonderful time together during that short period, but then once you both head back home, the relationship is over. Season relationships are wonderful gifts, and you either forget about the person after a short while or are left with a fond memory (and a smile on your face) for years to come.

A "reason relationship" occurs with an individual who happens to enter your life for a period of time and is there to teach you something, through either a good or a not-so-good experience. These relationships can be a catalyst for growth, happiness, pain, tragedy, helpfulness, or some other life lesson—they're in your life for a reason.

"Lifetime relationships" are the ones you have with your family. Relationships with your family last a lifetime, plain and simple.

Family Is Forever

You choose your friends based on similarities—you have similar tastes and you like similar things—but you don't have the luxury of choosing your family. You can interview people to fill a vacant position at work, but you can't interview to fill your mother's role. Family is what you're given. And just as you must make the most out of all the other things life gives you—your looks, your personality, your life experiences—you must make the most out of the family you've received.

Before there were therapists, support groups, and career counselors, there were moms, dads, brothers, sisters, and grandparents. Your family is the only connection you have to your heritage. You can end a friendship or a partnership and replace it with a new one, but you can't replace your heritage. Your family knows you like no one else does. They're part of your history, they raised you, and that relationship never ends.

Although I have many times been that spoiled boy who thought I didn't need relationships with certain members of my family, I am thankful to have been blessed with parents and siblings who forgave and still love me. I also have very clear benchmarks in my lifetime of when I was the one who chose to let go of a past hurt or misunderstanding and worked to rebuild a family relationship and reconnect where I'd thought I didn't need connection. With each of my family members, I can recite a chronological history, covering the past forty-plus years, of the dates, times, and experiences (those benchmarks) when I reconnected with those people. Although we may fall in and out of spending time together, sometimes for long periods of time, I know we'll eventually come back around, reconnect with each other, and establish the next level of our relationship. We do this over and over again, because these relationships fall into the category of lifetime relationships.

If we were to define maturity as our ability to function successfully in life in a healthy and productive way, then oh, how obvious it is that my maturity level closely mirrors and follows those benchmarks. When you find the frame of mind to work on those lifetime relationships with your family, your own maturity blossoms.

For all sorts of reasons—both valid and not—people sometimes choose to end relationships. I'm sure you've had family members do or say offensive things to you, and if a friend or employee acted the way the family member did, you'd have ended the relationship. But because it was family, you instead invested more—more love, more understanding, and more forgiveness. Because it was family, you eventually chose to let it go, heal the hurt, and move forward.

I thank God that I've chosen to let things go and move forward on many occasions with family members. I'm equally thankful that they chose to forgive me when I was foolish, because so many other wonderful experiences have taken place following the upset, and new and different relationships have unfurled.

Relationships Change

Because your relationships with family members last a lifetime, those relationships change many times, and they serve different purposes and meanings in your life. If you don't categorize your family members as lifetime relationships, you risk missing out on so much. You run the risk of closing out a lifetime relationship that could come back around later in life, provide you with growth and love, and prove to serve both you and the other individual involved.

I don't have the same relationship with my parents that I did ten years ago. And ten years ago, we didn't have the same relationship that we'd had ten years before that.

When I was in my twenties, my parents were my financial stability as I struggled to build a business and career. I remember a time back then when my selfishness could have blinded the importance of continuing to hold strong the relationship I had with them. Fortunately, my selfishness did not overbear my belief that family is a lifetime relationship.

When I was in my thirties, my parents were my emotional stability. I remember a time back then when my anger (whether valid or not) toward my parents' belief system clouded my conviction about the importance of my relationship with them. Once again, I'm thankful that my immature self did not destroy our relationship.

I'm now in my forties, and I view my relationship with my parents as a gift. I truly blossom when I'm fortunate enough to spend time with them. They provide substance, purpose, security, and centeredness. As my parents age and are faced with health issues, I believe that I can provide them with a sense of safety and caring.

Each of those relationship intervals has served me well and made me into the person I am today. Oh, how thankful I am that it was planted deep inside my being that my relationships with my parents and siblings aren't seasonal—they're for a lifetime.

How to Be Nice to Your Family

Family relationships can sometimes be the exact opposite of your relationships with co-workers. You might not love your co-workers but you have to like them, and you might not like your family but you have to love them. Easier said than done.

Because family relationships are lifetime relationships, you must constantly seek to improve and grow them. Unless you interject new beliefs, habits, or practices into your relationships, they become old, boring, or stagnant. Here are some ideas for bringing new life to your lifetime relationships.

Think Back

If you're married or in a significant relationship, think back to all those wonderful, romantic things you used to do for your spouse or partner while dating. I believe if everyone continued doing all those things, we wouldn't have the divorce rate in this country that we do. I find it very interesting that when people have an affair, they start doing all those romantic, wonderful things with the "new" person in their life. Just imagine what would happen if they went home and did them with their spouse instead.

"Pass or Fail" Exercise

I don't know about you, but I've found that on many days it's easier to smile at total strangers than it is to smile at that person at home. However, if you want a better relationship with your family, then you need to practice every day with total strangers. The curriculum I've designed for myself categorizes my experiences with others as either a "pass" or a "fail."

Imagine that in the course of one day you come across fifty people (some days it's more, some days it's less). The fifty people might include the total strangers you pass in the parking lot on your way in to work, the waitress in a restaurant, the bank teller, and the people you pass in traffic while driving to and from your work each day. What if you looked at all of those relationships as a "pass or fail" exercise?

You pass when you smile at that stranger in the parking lot, or you turn to someone on the elevator and say, "Have a nice day!" You pass when the waitress is in a bad mood and you go out of your way to cheer her up and make her laugh. You pass when another driver in traffic flips you off but you choose not to react at all.

You fail when you come across that stranger in the parking lot and do absolutely nothing at all. You fail when you stand on the elevator and just watch the floor numbers go by. You fail when perhaps that waitress has a worse day after her experience with you. Those are all categorized as big fat fails.

Here's a question to consider: Can you have fifty fails in a day, and then expect to go home and have a successful, constructive, positive, and loving relationship with your spouse or significant other? Absolutely not. You can't be a monster in the world and then expect to be charming at home. I can't help but think that people who scowl at total strangers must go home and scowl at their spouse, at their kids, and at the mirror.

Remember, if you want a better relationship with a spouse or significant other, if you want a better relationship with friends, co-workers, family members, or neighbors, then you need to practice all day, every day, with total strangers. Every stranger you encounter was sent to you "straight from central casting," as Marianne Williamson would say. They were sent to you for a very specific reason and purpose: They're your personal home-play assignments. So, which will it be—pass or fail?

Several years ago, I traveled to Cleveland, Ohio, with a dear friend of mine, Kitty Victor, for a two-day seminar we were facilitating together. After landing at the airport, we had a little more than an hour to grab our bags, take a taxi to the hotel, check in, change clothes, and begin the seminar. We jumped into a cab but didn't tell the driver that we were in a hurry. However, for some reason, our cabbie was driving like a maniac, and his driving was beginning to frighten us. He was driving fast, weaving in and out of different lanes, and was honking and yelling at other drivers who weren't even in his lane. A driver in the lane next to us was talking on his cell phone, which for some reason really angered our driver, so he sped up, cut in front of the driver with the cell phone, and then slammed on his brakes—all in rush-hour traffic.

At this point I yelled out to our driver, "What are you doing?" He mumbled something about the other driver talking on the phone and how he hated that. I angrily quipped, "Oh, so you're going to teach this other driver a lesson at the expense of our safety? Quit driving like a maniac! Slow down, and get us to our hotel safely."

At that point, Kitty turned to me and asked, "Pass or fail?"

What was my response? "PASS!"

You see, to improve your relationships and learn how to be a decent, nice person doesn't mean becoming a doormat for people. It doesn't mean letting people walk all over you while you bite your tongue. Unconditional love doesn't mean unconditional *abuse*.

Had I said nothing to the cab driver, would that have been a pass? No, because I wouldn't have been honoring the most important relationship I have: my relationship with myself. Had I physically or verbally attacked him—"You're an idiot and the worst driver in history!"—would that have been a pass? Again, no. Instead, what I did was something I call "clearing" with him, and in my book that's a pass.

Let's Be Clear

I used to believe that if I ever had a grievance, an opposing opinion, or a legitimate complaint with someone, I had to bite my tongue in order to be perceived as a nice guy. On those rare occasions when I did choose to tell the person how I felt or how they'd wronged me, I felt as though I was attacking them. Even if I wasn't really attacking, the fact that I had a grievance to share felt like an attack. And I'm not the attacking type, so I learned to keep it to myself, all locked inside. If you believe in a mind-body connection, as I firmly do, thanks to Louise Hay, you know that bottling things up and keeping them inside leads to stress, uneasiness, and dis-ease.

If you want to cultivate better long-term relationships with family, loved ones, new friends, and acquaintances, you're obviously going to have your disagreements and do the wrong thing on occasion. To keep from making yourself unhealthy, and to make sure your relationships grow and flourish, you need to practice being clear with people. Here are some guidelines.

▣ Keep It Between the Two of You

In high school, you'd get four friends on "your side" by telling them about the horrible thing someone else had done to you. Then you'd go to that person and say, "You're an idiot, and they all agree with me!"

Don't allow little battles to interrupt the sanctity of your lifetime relationships. It's so easy to divide a household with the tiny, seemingly insignificant comments you make about other family members. In the small confines of a family home, you must be aware of all your words, actions, moods, and attitudes, because every other family member could easily be placed in awkward and uncomfortable positions trying to keep peace and harmony.

▣ Always Clear Privately

When clearing with someone, always do it privately, where no one else can hear. If anyone else is there when you share and clear, the person you're clearing with will feel ganged-up on and attacked, and will therefore feel the need to defend themselves. One-on-one feels like communication from a friend and loved one. Two-on-one feels like a firing squad.

▣ Stick to the Facts

Only share with the person the actions and words that upset or hurt you. Let's say the person said something mean or unflattering about you at a party. Unless the person *always* says mean things about you in public, this was just a case of them being human, and perhaps it was an isolated incident. Rather than making the statement, "You're such a mean person," simply describe how you felt when you heard their comments about you in front of people.

▣ Focus on Your Desired End Result

It's human nature to want to focus on what the person did or said that hurt or wronged you, but where will that get you? Instead, decide in advance what the best possible outcome would look and feel like.

Sometimes you'll be tempted to rehearse a horrible outcome in your mind. You imagine yourself telling the person how they wronged you, and then you picture them firing back their defense and subsequent attack—you script and rehearse the entire negative, devastating scene, and it hasn't even happened yet.

As you plan to clear with a person, if you haven't decided what the end result is—or worse, if you've prewritten and rehearsed the end result to be one in which you were right and they were wrong—then your outcome will be "wrong." It won't matter how soft your voice is or what your physiology is as you clear with this person; your outcome will be a disaster. Instead, in advance, imagine the two of you talking it through, confirming your love and appreciation for each other, and ending the chat with a hug. Your end-result mantra could be:

> *You and I will be closer for having gone through this.*
> *I will honor myself and I will honor you as I clear with you.*
> *This experience is for our growth.*

It's Never Too Late

I loved the work I was able to do with author and counselor John Bradshaw's teachings, both through reading his books and attending his seminars. One of the things that he and many other mentors taught me is the profound value of doing the work to clear with people who've already passed on. Perhaps you didn't have a wonderful relationship with a parent and didn't have the chance to clean things up between the two of you and say what you needed to say before that person died. That doesn't mean you can't do the work now.

Journaling and letter writing are two powerful exercises for expressing thoughts, beliefs, and intentions of the heart. I believe it was Marianne Williamson who taught me that it only takes one person to make the shift in a relationship that got off track. If one person (you) decides to heal and mend a relationship, the other person doesn't have to participate. In fact, even if the other person decides not to participate, the work that you do to make your apologies, forgive that person, forgive yourself, and express your love and gratitude can be all that is required to proclaim, *That relationship is healed. I can now move forward with peace, love, and resolve.*

Build an Extended Family

Families can be chosen as well as inherited. Your family can include blood relations as well as "adopted" ones. For example, you might have a stronger bond with a childhood friend than with a true blood sister. Or you may be an only child by blood, but by building an extended family, you can take pride in telling people that your family is enormous.

We all build extended families. We adopt people into our lives and families, and we choose to take care of and look after certain individuals as though they were our own parent, child, or sibling. I think that's amazing, and we should always look for ways to grow our extended families. Let me share some ideas on where to look.

There might be some people in your life with whom you've had weekly or even daily interaction for years, and yet you know nothing about them. After ten years of continuous, close proximity, they could suddenly disappear, and you'd be left thinking, *I knew nothing about them, and they knew nothing about me.* In your life, who are those people? A co-worker? A neighbor?

The same cleaning lady, Angelina, has come to my house each week for eight years. She's responsible, caring, funny, inquisitive—and she's *family.* Angelina has daughters and grandchildren at home, whom I always ask about. Likewise, she always asks about my parents, whom she's met several times over the years when they've visited from out of town. I miss Angelina when I travel, and she tells me that she misses me. I sincerely hope she knows (and I often tell her) that she can come to me for anything. I want her to know that although we're not blood related, and although we live different lifestyles, she has someone she can count on; she has someone who will watch out for her. That's what families do.

Gifts and Benchmarks

Since family relationships last a lifetime, that certainly gives people years and years of opportunity to see and experience both the best and worst of each other. Anyone can be charming for a season, but a lifetime is tough.

To stay charming over the long haul, I believe it helps to look for gifts and benchmarks in life. A gift is an experience—either personal or not—that causes you to reflect on what's important. Not that you must go through life looking for horrible, dramatic tales to bring perspective into your life, but it's important to recognize those experiences for their significance when they do present themselves naturally. Again, these experiences are gifts, and they can become benchmarks in your life when they represent turning points of growth and change.

Following a bad experience, such as a home burning down in a neighborhood or the funeral of a loved one, people often say, "It's so sad that something like this had to happen for us all to come together." But the thing is, the experience *did* bring people together.

How many times have you watched the news on television and heard the devastating stories of parents losing a child? Hearing those stories brings tears to your eyes, helps you to appreciate your own family, and may cause you to tiptoe into the bedroom of your own sleeping children to give them a kiss and to stand there and stare with a new sense of love and appreciation. Though someone suffered by losing a loved one, you can consider these moments as gifts of life. They're gifts to you because they remind you to stop, take inventory of what's important, and renew your love and appreciation for your own family.

Remember, these experiences are gifts, and if you choose to give them value and awareness, they can be benchmarks for change in your life. I think of benchmarks in terms of before and after— "Before this happened, I didn't appreciate my weekends with my children, but now I do."

I was recently given one of life's gifts that I'd like to proclaim as a major benchmark in my life. My very dear friends from Houston, Sandy and Rosie, were blessed with a beautiful baby boy named Steel, born nine weeks premature. Although Steel was able to grow, develop, and even come home from the hospital for two months, he eventually took a turn for the worse and passed away, only three and a half months old.

The gift that Sandy, Rosie, and Steel gave to me was in allowing me to be a part of all of it—the excitement of Rosie's pregnancy, the struggle to make Steel grow strong, and the celebration of his young life after he died. Yes, sharing the experience of his death and funeral was a gift. Why? Because I grew more through all of that than I could have by attending a thousand seminars. The entire experience, sad as it was, proved to be a major benchmark in my life and has instantly put everything into perspective for me. Without sounding too dramatic, I can categorize my life as "Before Steel" and "After Steel."

Sandy and Rosie asked me to speak at little Steel's funeral, and this is what I said:

> For Sandy, Rosie, and Steel,
>
> I am not at all a churchgoing religious man. I am, however, a very spiritual man. I define my spirituality in terms of my peace of mind, my love of myself and my friends, and my sincere desire to be nice, do the right thing, and give back to those who are less fortunate than I. I do not attend a church or a synagogue in order to learn, practice, and exercise the beliefs that sustain my spirituality. Instead, I practice every single day by investing time and love into relationships.
>
> My altar is a quaint little table in a fabulous restaurant with amazing food, sharing a bottle of wine with people I love. I've shared that spiritual experience with Sandy and Rosie many times. My altar is in sharing and keeping embarrassing secrets with each other. We've shared those secrets with each other. My altar is in scheming to do a fun business project with someone that I meet and instantly like. Sandy, Rosie, and I have been scheming since we first met.
>
> I believe that spirituality is a very personal thing, that there are thousands of genuine spiritual paths, and that each of us has the responsibility and the adventure of discovering

the path that works for us. My spiritual beliefs tell me that communication doesn't end at death. Steel is still broadcasting. It's just that he is now on Channel 4, and you're still watching Channel 5. My challenge to you, Rosie and Sandy, is to hold on tight to each other, be listening and watching, because Steel is communicating with you.

To Sandy,

Perhaps you feel cheated as a father—that you didn't get the chance to love, support, and protect your little boy for a lifetime. But I'm here to tell you that you've played that role for many people. When I watch you interact with the hundreds of students at my school, or participate with them backstage at one of the students' fashion shows—yes, your stature gives people protection and safety, but your heart and love give young students hope and confidence.

To Rosie,

To see you last July as you showed that little belly of yours, while gleaming from ear to ear with the declaration of pending motherhood, I instantly forgave you for the red wine stain that is still visible on my white living room couch. That red wine stain happened because you were passionately telling a story while your hands were flying with expression. Please know that that passion is why many people choose you as their friend and mentor. It's probably why Sandy chose you to be his wife, and it's why Steel chose you to be his mother.

I've thought a lot about what this all means, and here's what I came up with. I have this very vivid and strong visual of Sandy, Rosie, and Steel meeting together many thousands of years ago in another place, discussing the relationship they'd have together on this earth, in this lifetime. And if you consider this life as a time to learn and grow, then my visual of Steel is him telling Sandy and Rosie, "You both need to be on Earth for about eighty-plus years to learn everything you need to learn. I only need to be there for a couple of months."

You see, all I can come up with is that Steel was so perfect that he really didn't need to be here on this earth for very long.

He came here, he taught his parents about a love they'd never experienced before, and then he moved on. It's not a tragedy, it's a gift.

I didn't get to meet little Steel, but I know and love his parents. Sandy and Rosie, when you're in pain, I'm in pain. When you cry, I cry. When you want to think and reminisce about Steel, I'll be your captive audience. And when you're ready to laugh again, please know that I want to be there, too.

All my love, Winn

Every Gift Can Become a Benchmark

By the way, the gifts that can be turned into benchmarks don't always need to be devastating, horrible happenings. They can be happy events, like birthdays. For example, you could use turning forty as an occasion to make proclamations about where you've been in life and what you've learned, to claim what you're grateful for, and to declare that you will now move forward.

On two occasions, I've awoken from a powerful, meaningful dream and have forever since proclaimed those dreams as benchmarks that changed my life. Both dreams were "visits" from loved ones who'd passed on. One was from a friend who'd taken his own life; his visit gave me the peace of mind that he was happy and doing fine. The other dream was a blissful and loving embrace from my grandmother.

Some might say, "Oh Winn, those were only dreams. It's wishful thinking that those were visits from loved ones." My response to that would be that *everything* in life is wishful thinking. The hope that your family will be safe is wishful thinking. Your desire to advance in your career is wishful thinking. Tell me what in life is *not* wishful thinking. I could shrug off those two visits, and think, *Don't be silly, Winn. They were only dreams.* But what good is there in believing that? What purpose would there be in talking myself out of those incredible feelings I had when I woke up? Instead, I've chosen to give strong meaning to those dreams. I consider them to be gifts, and I'm a better person simply because I woke up, said, "Thank you, God," and then turned those gifts into benchmarks. I try hard to recognize those benchmarks and blessings in my life, because they turn me into a different, better person.

Learning through Others' Experiences

Years ago, soon after it opened, I went with two friends of mine to visit the United States Holocaust Memorial Museum in Washington, D.C. I can't tell you how moved I was as I made my way at my own pace, reading, studying, and witnessing the history of such horrific crimes. I remember feeling completely numb in certain areas of the museum, and sobbing in other areas, such as in the room with the thousands of shoes, remnants from the hundreds of thousands of people who'd been exterminated in the death camps.

Two hours later, when we eventually departed from that solemn place, each of us having toured and experienced it on our own, I noticed something quite unique. My two friends were absolutely devastated. They described their experience as horrific, and they both felt incredibly depressed by it.

I, on the other hand, left the museum feeling more focused than I'd felt in years. I felt aligned, purposeful, and grateful for my freedom and my loved ones—I felt alive. Absolutely, the history shared there is devastating and one that none of us should ever forget or repeat. But I think that's the point: The reason the museum exists is not so that people are depressed, but rather so that we learn and grow.

A portion of the museum's mission statement confirms that purpose:

> The United States Holocaust Memorial Museum is America's national institution for the documentation, study, and interpretation of Holocaust history, and serves as this country's memorial to the millions of people murdered during the Holocaust. . . . The Museum's primary mission is to advance and disseminate knowledge about this unprecedented tragedy; to preserve the memory of those who suffered; and to encourage its visitors to reflect upon the moral and spiritual questions raised by the events of the Holocaust as well as their own responsibilities as citizens of a democracy.

You can wait for your own personal tragedies, or you can choose to learn from other people's experiences. All good learning experiences usually come with an assignment or home-play activity to make sure that you do indeed learn the lesson. Don't let experiences pass you by.

Write a Gratitude Letter

There are things that happened to you in the past that you may wish to forget. Even if you've voided out the pain of those experiences, you can go back and turn them into benchmarks—make your proclamation of what they meant to you, what you learned, what you lost, what you gained, and how you will be different. I'm not saying you have to relive the pain and emotion attached to the experience, but you can relive the experience in order to extract the gift.

One way to turn experiences into benchmarks is through letter writing or journaling. By writing it all down, it's almost as if you've proclaimed,

This event will not be in vain!

Remember in chapter 2, I shared some ideas about joy and pain. If you recall, I said that these two emotions motivate you, and you either do something because you believe it will bring you joy or you avoid it because you believe it will be painful.

I believe that you can learn certain lessons in life through either joy or pain. For example, you can choose to forgive someone now through a curriculum of joy, or you can refuse to forgive them and experience a curriculum of pain later, when you're filled with regrets and remorse. The curriculum of pain could be that the person you refuse to forgive passes away before you heal. The curriculum of joy can be as simple as reflecting on the experiences and gifts of life that you casually passed over without turning them into benchmarks, and taking time to write a gratitude letter.

Someone challenged me to make my gratitude letters a yearly birthday tradition, and I have done so many times. There's something quite profound and empowering about sitting down and making a list or writing a story about what's *right* in your life. Your gratitude letter can begin with a mention of the most obvious things you're grateful for, such as family and friends. You could write about the gifts of your heart, mind, and soul. You could express gratitude for worldly possessions, such as your car, your home, or a cookie jar given to you by your grandmother. I always like sharing gratitude for personal discoveries, benchmarks, and growth. Even if a painful experience helped me to be a better person or to appreciate my family more, I like showing gratitude for that experience and the lessons I've learned.

Although it can be very powerful and self-actualizing to write your gratitude letter and file it away in a journal for your eyes only, I've always chosen to mail copies of my letters to friends and family, and even to casual acquaintances. Some years I mail out ten copies of my gratitude letter, and other years I've mailed out over a hundred.

Here's the letter I wrote on my fortieth birthday several years ago:

April 8, 1999

Today I'm turning forty, and I couldn't be happier about it. So, to validate my feelings and beliefs, and in the tradition of writing my birthday letter, here it is.

It is important to point out that I am in Maui. This is one of my favorite places in the world (next to Laguna Beach), so this is where I wanted to spend this day.

It's amazing the comments that some people make when they find out about your upcoming "big four-oh." I can honestly say that I have not had one second of remorse about turning forty. In fact, I wouldn't want to go backward to a younger age for anything in the world, and I'll tell you why. Age has given me some "gifts" that I give thanks for often. They are few, so this will be short, but they are monumental.

The first gift I've noticed a lot recently is my high regard for elderly people, and I can honestly say that I didn't have this intense appreciation in recent years past.

I was recently in Scottsdale, Arizona, driving myself back to the airport. There was a man swerving around traffic, who, after passing me came upon an elderly lady who was going much slower than everyone else and had blocked him from passing. He laid on his horn, threatened her by getting closer to her car, and continued this for several miles. I can't tell you how upset I was by how this man, in my eyes, was violating and disrespecting this elderly lady. I didn't feel sorry or pity for her. I simply felt genuine respect and was therefore upset at how she was being treated.

Since my brother's death this past year, I've been reminded of certain feelings and practices to which I've again become committed. The most important is my relationship with my family. I am so grateful for the relationship I have with my parents. I enjoy them so much, and I can honestly say that I think about them every single day.

A couple of weeks ago I had a run-in with a family member and was quite upset and angry at this person for days. After a couple of days, it just dawned on me to pick up the phone and say, "It doesn't matter because we love each other."

When I told a friend, who knew the story of the temporary falling-out, that I had made the call, she said, "It must have been difficult for you to make that call." Without even thinking about it I replied, "Not making the call was difficult. Holding onto all that anger was difficult. Making the call was a piece of cake." I'm grateful at this point in my life that it's more natural for me to feel incredible love and appreciation for my entire family.

I said I was going to keep this one short, so bottom line is this: I have the career that I want—one that provides me with opportunities and experiences for growth and happiness beyond my wildest dreams. I have the business partnerships that I want with people I not only admire for their passion and expertise, but with people that I love. I own the type of business I want, where the entire focus is growth, learning, and self-improvement. I have the staff that I want to run that business, people who can see me at my worst, not freak out that the business will therefore go under, and slap me back on track. I have the energy that I want (I wasn't this hyper as a child—it seems to get more intense as I get older), the energy to sustain me in multiple projects all at once. I have the future career opportunities that I want, working with projects and people that a couple of years ago would have seemed nearly impossible. I have the loving friendships that I want, friendships that are oftentimes very romantic in the sense that our feelings for each other and the expression of those feelings are more a part of our friendships than just hanging out with each other. I live in the city that I want, in the house that I want. And finally, I'm in the relationship that I want—one in which I am never bored, oftentimes challenged, and always with a sense that I am truly loved.

Love to you all,

Winn

At this point, you might be thinking, *But Winn, I don't like to write,* or *I don't have time for a big, long letter like that.* No problem. There are plenty of ways you can list and acknowledge all the wonderful things you have in your life.

The following example was widely circulated as an e-mail. I wish I knew who originated it so I could give the proper credit, because I love the approach this person took in turning burdens into blessings. Take a look and you'll see what I mean.

I am thankful:

For the teenager who's not doing dishes but is watching TV, because that means he's at home and not on the streets.

For the taxes I pay, because it means I'm employed.

For the mess to clean after a party, because it means I've been surrounded by friends.

For the clothes that fit a little too snug, because it means I have enough to eat.

For my shadow that watches me work, because it means I'm out in the sunshine.

For the lawn that needs mowing, windows that need cleaning, and gutters that need fixing, because they mean I have a home.

For all the complaining I hear about the government, because it means that we have freedom of speech.

For the parking spot I find at the far end of the parking lot, because it means I'm capable of walking and I've been blessed with transportation.

For my huge heating bill, because it means I am warm.

For the lady behind me in church who sings off key, because it means I can hear.

For the pile of laundry and ironing, because it means I have clothes to wear.

For weariness and aching muscles at the end of the day, because it means I've been capable of working hard.

For the alarm that goes off in the early morning hours, because it means I'm alive.

And finally, for too much e-mail, because it means I have friends who are thinking of me.

What could you put in your gratitude letter or gratitude list? When you stop to think about the good things in life, you'll feel nicer and be nicer.

No Regrets

This has become a sort of mantra for me—No Regrets. Your life's body of work is about collecting beliefs and emotions. A life full of regret is certainly not what you desire, so why not make the proclamation: No Regrets.

Like many, there was a time when I found myself clocking birthdays with more and more regrets. I regretted not having a good relationship with my father. I regretted my bitterness over pieces of my childhood. I regretted not taking advantage of certain opportunities. Too many regrets. Regrets are like old baggage; they weigh you down. Why not set yourself up and live your life so as not to have any regrets when it comes to your relationships with family members?

For many years, I was angry with my dad because he didn't accept me for who I was. I complained to a friend about this, but my friend challenged me by saying, "You don't accept your father for who he is."

My response was, "Huh?"

My friend continued, "You feel cheated and denied by your father for not embracing your lifestyle, but you haven't embraced his lifestyle and beliefs."

"But he's the parent, and I'm the child," I defended. "He's supposed to accept and validate me."

My friend diligently reminded me of my beliefs, such as *Only what you aren't giving could be lacking in any situation*, and that my father has a little boy inside of him who's always looking for love, acceptance, and validation—just like me.

My friend was right. I was the one who was not accepting my father for who he is. The minute I did—the minute I entered his world and became interested in what he was interested in—all of a sudden two things happened. First, it seemed as though my father became more interested in me. Second, I no longer felt the desperation of needing my father's acceptance. I grew up, let go of the unfair expectations, and felt as though I could approach each day with no regrets.

In the past several years, my father has struggled with a number of health issues. I can't tell you how grateful I am that he and I figured our stuff out years ago, before his health issues began. If my father were to be taken from me tomorrow, I can honestly and thankfully say that I would have no regrets.

Lifetime relationships pose ups and downs, loving and fighting. So how do you sleep at night with the thought that if a loved one were to be taken from you, you would have no regrets? Sometimes there's no sense to the drama and conflict in family relationships. Sometimes the only thing that makes sense is to respond with, "You're my father, and I love you. That's all that matters."

▣ ▣ ▣

Like many people, the tragic events of September 11, 2001 had a profound effect on me—another benchmark. What I used to think I knew completely changed on that day, and my life will be forever divided into two segments: "Before 9/11" and "After 9/11."

I think of the crewmembers killed, and the terror of the passengers during those horrifying flights. I think of the people on all the floors of those buildings. There are so many parts of that tragic story that you could choose to focus on—parts of the story that could make you angry, confused, and fearful. But I must say that the stories I've chosen to focus on are about those individuals who were either in the towers or on a plane, who suddenly knew they had a brief chance to make a phone call.

Now here's the deal: They didn't call their boss to say, "How dare you not give me that raise!" They didn't call an old enemy to fight it out one more time. None of those things mattered. They called someone they loved—most often someone they'd had a lifetime, family relationship with—and they had just one message: *I love you.* That was it. Nothing else mattered, and nothing more needed to be said.

▣

What does that all mean to me? Well, you and I are still here. We still have to drive in traffic, pay our bills, and live through life's daily experiences. Just when I think I'm having a bad day or I'm at the end of my rope, I think to myself, *I wasn't on one of those flights or in one of the buildings that day. My problems are minor, petty, and can be dealt with.* And while I've moved through life day after day since 9/11, I've thought about those people and replayed their stories in my mind over and over again—almost in tribute to the thousands of people who lost their lives that day. For me, they didn't die in vain, and I've learned the lesson. For now, today, I get it. No regrets.

Your Home-Play Assignment:

Write a Gratitude Letter

What are you grateful for in your life? What events do you want to remember? What gifts would you like to memorialize as benchmarks?

As you finish this chapter, I'd like to urge you to write a gratitude list or gratitude letter.

Your gratitude letter can begin with a mention of the most obvious things you're grateful for, such as family and friends. You could write about the gifts of your heart, mind, and soul. You could express gratitude for worldly possessions, such as your car, your home, or a cookie jar given to you by your grandmother. You can share your gratitude for personal discoveries, benchmarks, and growth. Or you may want to express gratitude for a painful experience that helped you to be a better person or to appreciate your family more.

Write your gratitude letter, and acknowledge the experience and lessons you've been given in life.

Being Nice in the World

"The growth of friendship may be a lifelong affair."
—Sarah Orne Jewell

O ne of my favorite speakers and authors about love and relationships is Leo Buscaglia, who taught and preached that we should
love everybody. I once heard him challenged at a seminar with,
"Everybody? You certainly can't love everybody!" Leo theatrically picked
up his imaginary clipboard and pen and said something like, "Okay,
whom should I remove from my list of people to love? Prison inmates?
Well, studies show that 90 percent of inmates were unloved and abused
as children, so I can't remove them from my list. They definitely need
my love. So, who else should I remove and exclude from my list?"

Leo was brilliant. He knew that being nice in the world is not only
for the world's benefit, it's also for your benefit. It's okay to be nice out
of your own self-interests. To close your heart to someone *might* cause
them pain, but it *definitely* causes you pain.

But I Didn't Mean to Be Mean

In the 1960s there was a popular saying: If you're not part of the solution, you're part of the problem. I believe that's so true, and it applies to
being nice. When someone says, "I didn't mean to be mean," I want to

respond, "Yeah, but you didn't mean to be nice, either." Just as darkness is the absence of light, maybe we could agree that meanness is the absence of nice.

In this day and age, with the planet on shaky ground, with racism running rampant, with fears of terrorism threatening everyone's safety and security, with ecological and spiritual challenges on everyone's list of concerns, with our peace of mind being held for ransom, it's not enough to be neutral, it's not enough to *not* have the intention of being mean. Being nice in the world means you must have the intention and the constant, consistent focus to be nice. And you must learn how to constantly and consciously expand your "circle of nice."

Your Circle of Nice

You're probably familiar with the term *circle of influence*. It refers to those individuals with whom you come in contact either once or on a regular basis. Everyone who has any interaction with you is in your circle of influence, even if that interaction is only a chance meeting for thirty seconds in an elevator. In other words, your circle of influence includes people you know and people you don't know—your newspaper carrier, your kids, your co-workers, the ticket taker at the movie theater, the person who busses tables at a restaurant, total strangers on the freeway, and everyone else who crosses your path.

Whether you're aware of it or not, and whether you take responsibility for it or not, you have an influence on total strangers who pass you on the sidewalk. Think of how it makes you feel when a charming stranger pays you a compliment or smiles and offers you a heartfelt, sincere, "Have a wonderful day." Yes, those chance meetings can be amazing gifts, and those simple gestures can make someone's day.

Your *circle of nice* is a slightly different concept; it includes everyone you've decided to treat nicely. In a BE NICE world, the ultimate ambition for each of us is to include in our circle of nice the same exact individuals as those in our circle of influence—both people we know and many we don't know.

How to Expand Your Circle of Nice

If you think you're going to learn how to be nice by reading about it, you're mistaken. Just as you don't work your muscles by reading about fitness, you don't learn to be nice by reading one book. You jump on that Stairmaster to work your muscles, and you practice with real people to learn to be nice.

Being nice requires study, application, practice, and *other people*. Without practice and interaction with real, live human beings, no amount of studying will make you a nice person. Human beings are to nice-training as weights are to bodybuilding.

Since this book is about taking action rather than just reading information, please pull out four blank pieces of paper and create the following four lists:

1. **Your current circle of influence.** This will be a lengthy list of anyone and everyone you come in contact with on a daily basis, even if you don't know their names and even if you don't actually speak to them.

2. **Your current circle of nice.** These are the individuals to whom you've already made a conscious decision to be nice.

3. **Your immediate goals: The people you want to add to your circle of nice right now.** These are individuals or groups of people with whom you have contact, but for some reason or another (maybe you didn't even think about it until you read this book), you haven't yet added them to your circle of nice, but it would be easy to do so.

4. **Your long-range goals: The people you want to add to your circle of nice in the future.** These are individuals or groups of people who are *not* in your circle of nice, and you aren't quite sure how to add them, or whether or not you even want to add them yet. (Hey, no guilt here. No one's a master yet. We're all amateurs in this BE NICE way of life.)

For example, your lists could look like this:

---

1. My current circle of influence:

My mom and dad

My spouse/partner

My secretary

My brother Robert

My brother Vince

My sister Rachel

My brother Eric

My neighbors Kelley and Ron

My neighbors Marsha and Rick

My newspaper carrier

My co-workers Chris, Donna, Kathy, Brent, and Darrell

The people I see at the gym every day

All the other drivers on the freeway

2. **My current circle of nice:**

My mom and dad

My spouse/partner

My secretary

My brother Robert

My brother Vince

My sister Rachel

My neighbors Kelley and Ron

The elderly lady I see at the gym every day

My co-workers Chris and Donna

3. **My immediate goals (people I want to add to my circle of nice right now):**

My newspaper carrier

My co-workers Kathy and Brent

All the people at my gym

> **4. My long-term goals (people I want to add to my circle of nice in the future):**
>
> My brother Eric
>
> My neighbors Marsha and Rick
>
> My co-worker Darrell
>
> All the other drivers on the freeway

List 1, your current circle of influence, is your template of opportunity. Use it as a sort of goal sheet: Relentlessly refer back to it and evaluate whether it's the same as list 2 (your circle of nice list). If there are fifty names or groups on list 1, then your ambition and aim could be getting fifty names or groups on list 2.

Now, grab list 2, your current circle of nice. Next to each person's name, make a list of the *actions* you take to care for these people. How do you let them know they're indeed included in your circle of nice? For example, your list could look like this:

> **2. My current circle of nice:**
>
> My mom and dad—I call them almost every day just to say hi, and I always end my phone conversation with "I love you."
>
> My spouse/partner—We have a "date night" every Friday evening.
>
> My secretary—I go out of my way to let him know I truly appreciate how hard he works to make me look good. I buy him lunch at least once a week.
>
> My brother Robert—Because he collects match-books, I'm always collecting them from restaurants for him.
>
> My brother Vince—At least one Saturday per month I invite his kids to join my kids and me on a family outing to give him and his wife a Saturday alone.

My sister Rachel—I've set up a college fund for her two young children to help her out.

My neighbors Kelley and Ron—I either take their garbage cans to the curb on trash day if they haven't already, or I bring them back to their house after trash pickup.

The elderly lady I see at the gym every day—I say hello to her every time I see her, and on occasion remind her to let me know if she needs a spotter to watch her as she lifts weights.

My co-workers Chris and Donna—At least once a month I bring lunch back to them when I see that they're swamped and can't leave for a lunch break. I also offer to pitch in whenever I see them stressed or behind in their work.

Be very specific as to what you do to take care of these people and how you let them know they're on your circle of nice list. Those very specific actions—even the little things you do—will come in quite handy as you attempt to grow your circle of nice.

Now look at list 3, the people you want to add to your circle of nice immediately. Adding people to the circle is easy—it only requires making the decision to do so. Until you began reading this book, it might not have occurred to you to stop your newspaper carrier, say hello, and offer him or her a cold drink, but now you can choose to do that. Perhaps it never occurred to you to say hi to everyone in the gym, the same as you do that elderly lady you see there every day. Perhaps starting now you'll consciously offer help to your other co-workers when they run behind, the same as you do for Chris and Donna. Who knows, maybe you'll even splurge on occasion and buy their lunch when they're swamped and can't leave for a lunch break.

The thing to remember about the people on list 3 is that you must make a conscious decision to take actions toward including them in your circle of nice. A conscious effort to take action again and again will eventually turn the action into a habit, and good habits form a beautiful character, personality, and disposition. You become adorable. So review list 3, and make the decision to add these people to your circle. Then, when the opportunity arises, you'll be ready to take action and let them know they're in your circle of nice.

Now look at list 4, the people you want to add long-range. This one may take some work, because you probably have a valid rationale as to why these people aren't already in your circle of nice. Maybe it's because they've done something to offend or hurt you. Yes, what other people do or say can feel hurtful. However, it's worth noting that anytime you close your heart to someone, it causes *you* pain. If you seek to open your heart more, you'll take this next step.

Since you don't have to save the world today, why not choose just one of the names on that list to drag over into your circle of nice? Perhaps it will be those annoying neighbors, Marsha and Rick, with whom you've been battling for years because they always play their music too loudly. Or maybe you'll choose that jerk at work, Darrell. Or maybe it's time to reach out to that distant brother, Eric.

The thing to realize here is that the simple gestures you offer to the individuals on list 3 might not be enough to bring these list 4 people into your circle of nice. Maybe the wounds run deep, or the past infractions can't be erased with a simple offering. Perhaps you'll have to work harder to make sure your actions toward these individuals have significant meaning, both to them and to you.

Not Everyone Belongs on the List

Please note: Perhaps to take care of yourself, and to keep your self-esteem and safety intact, there are some individuals you might need to keep at a distance. That's not only correct, valid, and proper, it's a requirement. Those individuals would include an abusive ex-partner or ex-spouse, or anyone who jeopardizes your physical or emotional safety or well-being. I stay away from certain people for the same reason I stay away from gossipy talk shows, violent movies, and spicy foods— because those things do not make me feel good about myself.

At one point in my life, I experienced a drug addiction problem, which I completely and totally believe is in my past, and for that I am both grateful and humbled. There were individuals in my life at that time whom I now choose not to be around. Is it because I'm judging them, or because I don't think they're good, nice people or worthy of my association? No, it's not for any of those reasons. It's simply because I'm not Superman. I can't save the world and everyone in it. I can only save myself, and I don't want to revisit the circumstances or the people in those circumstances that led to an unhealthy lifestyle. I take full responsibility for my actions and don't blame anyone, so please don't write me a letter about that.

My point is this: For whatever reason, there may be certain individuals with whom you have chosen not to spend time. In my experience of making those decisions and choices, some people have been quite hurt and even attacked me over my "divorce" from them. Their statements toward me have included, "You really aren't this wonderful, nice person you profess to be, or you'd return my phone call. Who do you think you are to judge me? You think you're better than me?"

Just because you don't include certain people in your circle of nice doesn't mean their accusations are true, and it doesn't mean you're not a nice person.

Cultivate a Colorful, Eclectic Circle of Friends

Look at your circle of friends. Do they represent a healthy cross section of people or are they all exactly alike, with the same interests, beliefs, lifestyles, and closed minds? Life is meant to be colorful, diverse, and dramatic. A sunset is filled with drama. A rainbow boasts a wide variety of colors. Leaves on a tree are as different as anything could be. Then why should your circle of friends be so drama-less and color-less?

Seek out friends or at least acquaintances who bring variety, perspective, and insight to your world. Open yourself up to friends of every gender, color, religion, heritage, sexual orientation, interest, belief system, and lifestyle. Not only will you expose yourself to fascinating cultures, you'll also liberate yourself from some of the negative beliefs that can accompany stereotypes.

Romance Your Friends

When it comes to the gifts we offer, many of us were taught to give certain gifts to some people and different ones to others. When I mention gifts here, I'm referring to levels of emotions, niceties, sentiments, and passions. For example, to your best friend and confidant, you might offer 80 percent of your gifts of fun and lightheartedness, but perhaps you'll give that person only 10 percent of your passion. To your spouse and lover, you may deny your lightheartedness (marriage is serious business!), but give full access to your passion.

Here's a radical notion: Treat your lover more like a friend, and treat your friends more like a lover.

I've been blessed with a circle of friends who are funny, talented, passionate, loyal, caring, and giving. How do I know they're all those things and more? Because we erased the boundaries and did away with the stiff constraints that dictate how we should and should not experience each other. Simply put, we chose to romance each other, even though several of us have spouses or partners of our own.

I love the nuance and awareness of the word *romance*. It implies a different purpose, motive, and mind-set for my thoughts and actions. In some ways, the notion of romance sets me free and offers more possibilities for expression, honesty, and support. Applying all of that to my platonic friendships has added immeasurable depth to my soul and has skyrocketed my confidence as I take on the world.

Look for opportunities to share romance with your friends. Usually, the opportunity to cultivate a romance with a friend will present itself in the exact same circumstance as it would with a lover. Here are some ideas I've gathered from my friends about what we do to cultivate our romance.

▣ Pamper Your Friends When They're Sick

This could be great news in the world of romancing your friends, because a lot of us digress into a childlike state when we're sick. We want to be pampered, taken care of, and shown that someone cares about our well-being. When the person knocking on our door with chicken noodle soup and a sappy '80s video happens to be one of our best friends, we're at first surprised, then eventually at ease and ever so grateful.

▣ Write Love Notes

This is one of my favorites. I can honestly say I receive at least one love note a week, from a circle of about ten friends. I also send out at least one love note per week. These love notes say more than just "Thank you for dinner," although dinner would be an occasion that warrants a love note. But why not spice up those nice little notes?

Why not include in your thank-you message a mention about something lovely that was shared in conversation in the course of the dinner? Your love note could include reminiscing about an endearing or pivotal experience in your friendship building with that person. Here's a brief example:

I'll never forget your lovely words of encouragement many years ago after I got fired from that horrible job. You captured my heart then, and you continue to capture my friendship every time I spend time with you.

I save many of the love notes I've received from my friends. I constantly carry a couple of them around with me in my planner, and I read them often, until they're replaced with a more recent note.

▣ Play Show and Tell

I'm always gathering "souvenirs" of my daily activities so I can share them with my friends the next time I see them. I show them my latest shoe purchase, an interesting magazine article, a cool e-mail from a long lost friend, a song that made me cry, or even a funny fortune from a fortune cookie. Maybe it's been a week or a month since I've seen that person, and during that period of time I've gone through all sorts of experiences and emotions. By playing "show and tell," I can relive some of those experiences and emotions, and share them with my friend.

▣ Give Gifts

We all love to receive a gift, especially when it's not even our birthday or a holiday. When I fall in love with a new music CD, I buy five extras to give to my romantic friends. I don't wait for a special occasion; the gifts are given randomly—just because. When I see a T-shirt with a funny message that completely captures one of my friends' personalities, of course I'm going to buy it for them. The gifts are sometimes expensive, but oftentimes just little memento items, such as a tiny picture frame with a snapshot of the two of us, or an inexpensive key ring in the shape of their pet dog. Other cool gifts to give to friends could include a photo album filled with pictures of your high school days, a recent vacation you took together, or their birthday party. Some circles of friends continually play practical jokes on each other, which can certainly be fun and friendship building, but romance might require more thoughtful offerings, such as a simple, unexpected gift.

◧ Respect Your Friends' Relationships, Even When You Don't Agree with Them

Having romantic friendships can be a bit tricky if you don't respect your friend's spouse or partner. You don't have to agree with the relationship, but you definitely must respect it. All relationships provide growth opportunities for the people involved, including those relationships that you don't agree with. Sometimes the biggest support you can give to a friend is to shut up about why you think their spouse or partner is an "idiot."

How to Be Nice to Service People

Some people seem to have the attitude that some individuals were born to serve, and others were born to be served. It's been my experience that those who've worked in a service capacity—in the hotel, restaurant, retail, or travel industries—tend to have compassion and generosity for those who might be serving them. I often notice that my hairdresser friends are the biggest tippers in restaurants.

Once again, this could just be a realization issue. Perhaps prior to reading this book, you were living out of ignorance and weren't conscious of the bad habit of not acknowledging people in the service business. Well, now that you know, it's time to go overboard and make up for all the times you ignored all those wonderful, amazing, humble, talented individuals who've made your life easier through their service. From now on, you can go out of your way to stop and say hello to the hotel cleaning person, the flight attendant, the restaurant table busser, the hotel clerk, the garbage collector, the gardener . . . Who have I left out here, and who have you left out over the years?

How to Be Nice in Your Community

We live in a colorful, diversified world. Because there are cultures, countries, traditions, and languages that are foreign to us, our ignorance can get in the way of presenting ourselves as nice, sensitive individuals.

Take time to educate yourself, so as not to be offensive by using the wrong terminology in referring to different races or ethnic groups. You might live in a tiny neighborhood, but you're a member of a world community—and our world is looking for some really good ambassadors. Be sensitive by using politically correct terms.

How to Be Nice to People Who Aren't Nice to You

It's easy to be nice when everyone's nice to you. It would be easy to be nice if you were never "flipped off," or yelled at by a stranger for no reason, or called a name, or made the victim of a racial slur. It would be easy to be nice while on vacation in Maui, where almost everyone is relaxed and away from the pressures of day-to-day life. But being a nice person in rush-hour traffic can be a bit of a challenge.

When someone isn't nice, you want to put them in their place. You want the last word, and you want to let them know of their infractions. As I shared earlier, there's nothing wrong with clearing with an individual whom you believe has wronged you. But there's another way to handle the situation so that you don't feel victimized and so you can preserve your peace of mind. How do you do that? By not even allowing the offensive comment or action to get in. You can do that by immediately changing your perception of the experience.

The thing to realize is that you choose your attitude in every situation. Perhaps you don't have much control over what happens to you in life, but you do have control over—and are therefore responsible for—your reaction to what happens to you. You're responsible for your experience of the experience.

How to Be Nice While Being Written Up for a Speeding Ticket

Okay, this could be a tough one, especially if you continue to live under that old paradigm of looking at the police as "them versus us." If you speed down highways and freeways, hoping no police officers are watching, those flashing red lights are probably the last thing you want to see. But if you were ever the victim of a robbery, a violent crime, or a traffic accident, who's the first person you'd want to see? That's right, the police.

Admit it, you've sped before, rolled through stop signs, and probably been guilty of many other traffic violations—and you've gotten away with it. The next time you get caught and you see those flashing lights in your rearview mirror, why not choose a different way to look at the situation?

First, remember that police officers are just doing their job, which is to keep you safe. If you like being safe, you probably want them to continue doing their job. You might even want to thank them for doing their job while you've got them for this captive audience. Second, consider yourself lucky for all the times you weren't ticketed and probably should have been.

If those two thoughts aren't enough to change your mood about getting a speeding ticket, here are a few BE NICE attitude adjusters to help you alter your angry state:

1. Tell yourself that the policeman or policewoman could be having a bad day, and the universe sent them directly to you to cheer them up.

2. Remind yourself that they're doing the best they know how to do in that instant, just as you are.

3. Tell yourself that the policeman or policewoman has a young, sick child at home. (This may or may not be true, but that's not the point. You're looking for quick attitude adjusters here.)

4. As the police officer approaches your window, quickly recite your BE NICE mantra, such as *Thank you God*, or *I like myself.* How about one from Louise Hay's book, *You Can Heal Your Life*, such as "I release the pattern in me that created this. I am at peace. I am worthwhile."

The bottom line here is that your speeding ticket interaction is actually a relationship with another human being. Remember that all relationships are pass or fail exercises. The more fails you have, the more times the universe will send you those same relationships and experiences (more speeding tickets) so that you can learn to get it right. The more passes you have, the happier you become.

How to Be Nice in Rush-Hour Traffic

Road rage is an epidemic that's sweeping the planet. How did this happen? Yes, it's crowded out there with billions of people living on Earth, but why is it that when we get into our cars we yell, think, gesture, and react in ways that are so completely opposite of our personality and nature? Without that metal box around us, we don't act that way in other crowded situations. Why do we do it when we climb into our cars?

My good friend Marianne is a wonderful and kindhearted person, but not long ago she caught herself acting totally out of character in a grocery store parking lot. She was ready to leave, but the exit was blocked by an SUV. The driver was waiting for her passenger to get into the car, but he was taking his good old time. He started for the passenger door, then went to the back of the car, opened the trunk, and started putting a package inside. Marianne was getting increasingly upset, thinking, *Why can't he just get in the car? Doesn't he know he's blocking my way?* Maybe ten seconds had elapsed, but she felt and acted like it had been half an hour.

Marianne sat there, cursing under her breath. She'd been under a lot of stress lately. Her father was sick again, her daughter was having problems, and Marianne's patience was pretty much shot. But then the driver looked at her—not because she could hear Marianne, but because she was genuinely sorry her passenger was taking so long. She held up her finger as if to say, "Just a minute," and mouthed the words, "I'm sorry." Suddenly, Marianne's anger disappeared and she felt, in her words, "like crap. It made me realize that this is some world where we can't wait ten seconds for a car to get out of our way." She smiled and waved, mouthing, "That's okay." And you know what? It really was okay.

The universe sees *everything*, so you can't expect to attract and retain loving relationships and supportive friendships if you allow yourself to turn into a monster on the road. You can't make disgusting gestures to strangers on the highway, and then expect to genuinely and graciously greet a customer with that same extended hand.

Road rage is a bad habit, and habits are meant to be broken. So, set yourself up to be nice in your car. Set yourself up to win. Here's how:

1. **Drive a clean car.** I know I've said this before, but it bears repeating. We all feel better about ourselves when we're driving a clean car, and yet we'll drive a dirty car for weeks. If you want to be nicer in your car, start by keeping it clean.

2. **Listen to motivational tapes and CDs in your car.** Your driving time can be valuable, private learning time for you if you turn

your car into a "learning facility." When else do you have the time to sit down with a great tape or CD without interruption? Turn your commute into private, sacred time for learning how to be nice, even if your commute time is only ten minutes. Ten minutes is enough to get your mind focused for the entire day.

3. **Listen to good music.** A lot of talk radio is designed to cause a rise and confrontational stir from its audience. That's how they get people to listen and call in. If you're already the type of person who has a challenge keeping harmony and love in your heart for your fellow drivers, listening to talk radio can be like squeezing lemon juice into a wound. When you're surrounded by "a bunch of idiots who will *never* drive as well as you do," why would you want to listen to talk radio, whose job it is to validate your belief that "people are idiots"? Turn off that radio! If motivational tapes and CDs aren't your style, then choose music that inspires you, calms you, soothes you, and makes you happy.

4. **Drive different routes every once in a while, just to break up the monotony.** If your drive to and from work turns into a discovery, rather than a rut and a routine, your emotions will not go south.

5. **Place a photograph of your kids, your spouse, or your partner next to the steering wheel.** Imagine how much road rage could be eliminated if drivers were seeing the face of a loved one while spewing their toxic insults to fellow drivers.

6. **Find fun and interesting ways to be nice to your fellow drivers.** Several years ago, my friend Debra had just moved to the San Francisco Bay area. One day, as she went to pay the toll for the Bay Bridge, she received a pleasant surprise—the truck driver ahead of her had paid the toll for her. Touched by the unconditional generosity of this total stranger, Debra decided to adopt his behavior as her own. Ever since that day, every time she crosses the bridge, she pays the toll for the person behind her. She does it even when she has no spare change, and she does it because it "felt good" when someone did it for her. Road rage? Not in Debra's car.

How to Be Nice to the Elderly

In the 1970s there was a television comedy show called *Mork and Mindy*. Mork, an alien from another planet, lived on Earth with Mindy to learn about earthlings. At the end of each episode, Mork would contact his planet and report back to his commanding officer. His observations would usually deliver a positive moral.

At the end of one episode, Mork's message went something like this: It's very strange that people here on Earth value most anything that is old. They value old wine, old furniture, old paintings, and so on. The one old thing that Earthlings don't value is old people.

I've grown to love and appreciate elderly people. If I chose to, I could recognize and dwell on their negative, crotchety character traits—traits that, by the way, also exist in young people. However, I find elderly people to be cute, funny, wise, and grateful, and they possess the best manners. That's what I choose to see, and so my experience with the elderly is always filled with joy and respect.

Okay, so old people might move slower and drive slower. So do you and I, on occasion. In order to show my love and respect for the elderly, and so that I can harness my rude, impatient self when I'm stuck behind a slow-moving senior, here's what I do. I pretend that the slow-driving old lady in front of me is my own mother or grandmother. I would *never* lose patience with or honk at my own mother or grand-mother, and I certainly wouldn't want total strangers to lose their patience and honk at them, either.

Just remember that the universe has eyes. Your own self-love and confidence are undeniably tied to what you put out there. Honking at an old lady to get her out of your way may help you arrive at your destination five minutes sooner, but the devastation you inflict on that old lady will set you back in ways you can't even comprehend. To truly be nice in the world, let's love, honor, and respect our elderly. After all, we're all on our way there someday, too.

He's Not So Nice

Once you make the proclamation that you're a nice person, be prepared for the line to form of people who will say you're anything but nice. When you tell someone you're committed to a life of being nice, be prepared for the comments: "I went to high school with that guy, and he was *not* nice!" You'd think that being nice would bring out the best in others, and for the most part it does. But sometimes, it's like showing up to work really happy—have you ever noticed how that can really upset some people and bring out the worst in them? Instead of joining your good mood, they ask, "What are you so happy about?"

All I can say to that (and the advice I give to myself) is, stay strong. Anything worthwhile is a struggle and takes work, and that applies to building your reputation as a nice person.

What If Someone's Mean to You?

Let's face it, unless we're chronically cruel, we usually display our not-so-nice behavior when we're tired, stressed, lazy, or just having an off day. Since most people are like you and me, we can assume that another person's not-so-nice behavior is due to the same reasons we act that way.

I used to have the attitude that if someone was in a bad mood and therefore treating people "not nice," they should just get over it. However, I've since learned how easy it is to defuse a person's bad day or bad mood, and since some very generous people have done that for me on occasion, I figure I can make it a good habit and practice doing the same for others whenever I see the opportunity.

How to Defuse People

Everyone occasionally gets trapped in a bad mood for one reason or another, and their bad moods can lead to bad actions. Defusing people is all about giving them a dose of something that could alter their mood or thinking.

My very good friend Kate calls herself an "emotional fluffer-upper." Sometimes it's just her *Flintstones* Betty Rubble laugh that's enough to defuse a person. Other times she's very specific and calculating about how she goes about fluffing someone's self-esteem and attitude.

On occasion, Kate will stop me dead in my bad-mood path, grab me by both shoulders, shake me until I look her in the eye, then ask, "What exactly can I do right now as your emotional fluffer-upper to make you feel better? What do you need *right now?*" Let me tell you something—

it works. Sometimes all I need is to know that someone recognized that I was stuck and was willing to help me get unstuck.

A friend told me the story of a man on his airplane flight who was in a miserable, complaining mood. When the flight attendant served him his in-flight meal, he quickly handed it back with a comment about how bad the sandwich was. The flight attendant didn't skip a beat. She took the sandwich, shook her finger at it, and declared, "Bad sandwich! Bad sandwich!" I don't remember my friend saying whether or not the man was defused of his bad mood, but I know it would have defused me.

In business, the best and easiest way to defuse a complaining, irate customer is *not* to make excuses or to place blame for the circumstances that made the customer upset. Even if there was an excuse, and even if you could place blame, angry customers rarely care about the reasons. The best thing to do is to let them vent, let them get it all out. Once they've done that, you need only say, "I'm so sorry you were inconvenienced. What wonderful thing could I do to make you happy?"

I once had one of those awful flying experiences where flight after flight was delayed, and none of the delays were weather related. What should have been a three-hour flight turned into a fifteen-hour, multiple-city, exhausting nightmare, causing me to miss meetings in my intended city. At 3 A.M., by the time I was finally within thirty minutes of landing at my destination airport, I suddenly smelled something wonderful. The flight attendants were baking chocolate chip cookies! That sweet, comforting aroma filled the airline cabin, and our small group of twenty passengers waited with anticipation as the flight attendants made their way down the aisle, handing each of us a warm cookie. I instantly abandoned my plans for an enraged letter-writing campaign against the airline and was effortlessly defused of all my anger and exhaustion—all by one soft, freshly baked cookie.

◼ ◼ ◼

Remember, in a BE NICE world, the ultimate ambition for each of us is to make our circle of nice the same exact individuals as our circle of influence—both the people we know and many we don't know. If you didn't complete the circle of nice exercises as you read through this chapter, please follow the home-play assignment instructions and do it now. This is one of the best and most rewarding assignments you'll ever do.

Your Home-Play Assignment:

Expand Your Circle of Nice

Pull out four blank pieces of paper and create the following four lists:

1. **Your current circle of influence.** List everyone you come in contact with on a daily basis, even if you don't know their name or actually speak to them.

2. **Your current circle of nice.** These are the individuals to whom you've already made a conscious decision to be nice. Next to each of these names, list the *specific* actions you take to care for these people. How do you let them know they're included in your circle of nice?

3. **Your immediate goals: The people you want to add to your circle of nice right now.** List the individuals or groups of people with whom you have contact but haven't yet added to your circle of nice. Make a conscious decision to take actions toward including them in your circle of nice.

4. **Your long-range goals: The people you want to add to your circle of nice in the future.** These people are *not* in your circle of nice, and you aren't quite sure how to add them, or whether or not you even want to add them yet. Choose one person to begin moving into your circle of nice.

Being Nice in the Workplace

"No member of a crew is praised for the rugged individuality of his rowing."
—Ralph Waldo Emerson

hen it comes to the workplace, BE NICE is a marketing campaign, a boardroom strategy, a staff training theme, and a customer promise. BE NICE is part of a company's mission statement and vision, a focus for the staff holiday party, and a philanthropic promise to the community. It will increase staff morale and loyalty, improve customer service, and at the same time increase profits. Why? Because customers will spend a lot of money with a company that's nice. The company that embraces a BE NICE culture has a major competitive edge. BE NICE is not just a platitude, it's good business.

A good friend of mine who's also a successful attorney recently planned a dinner party in her home for a large group of friends and business associates. She ordered engraved invitations, flowers, catering, live music, a car valet, and more. As my friend made arrangements with business after business, she noticed that some of her experiences were pleasurable and some were not. She said that the painstaking process of ordering the invitations—choosing the paper, the font, the color of the ink—was a wonderful and fun experience, whereas the simple, onetime visit to the bakery to order gourmet desserts gave her an awful, "how dare you interrupt my day" type feeling from the bakery employee. With which company do you think my friend will continue doing business?

Can you imagine a company with a motto of "BE MEAN"? Of course not. But the absence of a strong mission statement and campaign to create a BE NICE culture will, by default, create a mean one. If you're not consciously and actively choosing and pursuing BE NICE in your organization, then you're choosing BE MEAN. You can't hang out somewhere in the middle. There's not much gray area here, nor is there room for a wishy-washy, spineless resolve like, "We're pretty nice, sometimes, when we have to be."

I believe that all organizations, companies, businesses, stores, and family units must consciously and actively adopt and promote the beliefs and practices of being nice.

A company or organization that conveys the opposite of being nice, or even settles for "Be unsympathetic, uncaring, heartless, unconcerned, insensitive, or indifferent" can sit back and watch staff loyalty diminish and profits decrease. As the people at Disney might say, heaven help the business that isn't nice.

A couple of years ago, I overheard one of my new staff members on the phone being impatient and a bit rude. When I told him to be fun and nice on the phone, his comment was, "I usually am, but I'm really busy right now." I thought, *What does being busy have to do with being nice? How much extra time does it take to change the tonality of your voice, so people know they're dealing with someone who is nice?*

Make no mistake—your customers are attracted to you more by your enthusiasm than by your marble floors; more by your cheerful disposition and love for what you do than by your sleek business cards; more by your company standards for respecting human beings than by your multimillion-dollar advertising campaign. When you make BE NICE a daily priority, your company or business will reap the rewards.

Being Nice Is Everyone's Responsibility

If you glanced ahead at this chapter and saw words such as *leader, owner,* or *manager,* and you do *not* possess any of those titles, that doesn't mean you're exempt from studying and implementing the information shared here. Leadership is not a position, it's a mind-set and an attitude. If your mind-set and purpose are to be nice, then your position and title won't matter, because you can provide more effective leadership than the big guy or gal in the big office.

I'm sure you'll agree that sometimes the brand-new employee who's only worked at the company for a few months and is at the bottom of the totem pole can do more for building morale, teamwork, and niceness than people who've worked there for twenty years or more. *Everyone* in a company, corporation, office building, store, or business must assume responsibility for its overall success. Here's a great philosophy to live by:

What's good for the company is good for me.

For the record, it's not just the customer service department's job to be nice. The employees who handle payroll can do damage and destroy company morale and the good feelings necessary to make a business function successfully. Every individual—from CEO to janitor, from accountant to salesperson—must heed the call to be nice. However, it's a lot easier to be nice when you're part of a BE NICE culture and community.

The best way I know to share the information in this chapter, so your company or organization can make BE NICE a part of your culture and community, is to first share with you a little information about cultures and communities, and then examine the behaviors that need to be ever-present. These behaviors come from values, which lay the foundation for a strong community of happy, loyal, hardworking, passionate employees who, in turn, attract more employees who possess those same qualities and traits. A company filled with those types of employees attracts and retains happy, loyal customers.

Creating a BE NICE Culture and Community

Having a "job" means working for a place where there's no consistency, no fun, no sense of family, no sense of purpose, no sense of belonging—and no culture or community. You can walk into a store or business where twenty staff members all work for the same company, all theoretically have the same purpose and goal, and yet it may seem like twenty separate, individual, independent little businesses are going on. There's no consistency, no teamwork, no communication, no support for each other, and a catastrophic it's-not-my-job attitude. Do you think the customer picks up on that? Do you think the customer wants to continue spending money in that type of a business?

Similarly, you could walk into two different companies that produce the exact same product or service, and yet one company feels contaminated and unappealing while the other feels comfortable and welcoming. Is it because employees working for Company A just happen to be more negative and gossipy than the employees at Company B? Hardly. But without a culture, people are just "hanging out." People just hanging out has never been a good thing. I believe we call it loitering.

When applied to the business world, a *culture*, by definition, is a set of shared attitudes, values, goals, and practices that characterize a company or corporation. A *community* is more inclusive of anyone and everyone. It's defined as a unified body, or a people with common interests. Although individuals may have different backgrounds, beliefs, and lifestyles away from work, when they all come together in a workplace community, the goal is to get them on the same page, believing in the same purpose, and striving for a common end result.

By the way, I don't believe that you *find* good people to come work in your company—you *attract* good people. You don't steal good people away from your competitor; instead, you create a culture and build a community that attracts good people, and then together you work hard to develop each other.

Visionary, Fence Sitter, or Resister: You Choose

People in a workplace community can most likely fall into three different categories: visionary, fence sitter, or resister.

Visionaries are people who've caught the vision of the company— they make things happen. For them, it's not just about the paycheck. They never have that it's-not-my-job attitude. They respect all job descriptions, protocols, and company standards. They do whatever it takes to make sure the company is profitable, the team is happy and healthy, and their participation is for the good of everyone. Their attitude is, "What's in it for *us* today?" We love these people. Don't get confused into thinking that a visionary must be a person in upper management, or someone who's been with the company for a long time. You can be brand-new, be the lowest paid person, and still be a visionary.

Fence sitters are people who, on any given day and with any given project, could go either way. Some days they're for you, some days they're against you. As a business owner, I sometimes stand at the door watching my staff members arrive, and think to myself, *I wonder which way that person will go today.* Fence sitters easily succumb to human emotions. Their loyalty and commitment are tied to their mood that day, or to some other arbitrary scale. If their second moon is rising over Jupiter, then they love working for the company. But when their Uranus is stuck and dragging out of bed that day, forget about it!

Resisters think it's their job to resist *anything* and *everything.* If you could look up their self-imagined job description, it would probably say, "Resist, resist, resist!" You say "black," they say "white" . . . *just because!* Resisters are very good at planting their insidious seeds of negativity. They'll be out having cocktails with other staff members, and while discussing the staff meeting held earlier that day, they'll say something like, "Wasn't that a great speech that so-and-so gave today? But did you hear about her marital problems?" They plant that negative seed, and then move on to the next project or person to resist and sabotage.

It's important to identify your visionaries, fence sitters, and resisters so you'll know where to invest your energy and time. How do you handle these three different types of people? Unfortunately, in many companies and organizations, all the attention goes to the resisters (the squeaky wheel gets the oil), while the visionaries quietly work away, ignored and unappreciated.

Take heed: Ignore the resisters. Don't let them set your agenda. Without showing disrespect, avoid giving them your attention, your focus, or your energy. It's true that positive behavior will disappear if you ignore it, but so will negative behavior. And when I say disappear, I mean either the resisters will leave your company to move on to one that tolerates and condones their negativity, or their behavior will change. And by the way, if their behavior doesn't change, SW, SW, SW! Some will, some won't, so what!

Now about those visionaries—*listen up!* They need your attention. They need your praises, your hugs, your pats on the back, and your public displays of meaningful gratitude. They need for you to put them on a pedestal and let everyone know that they make a difference in your world. In fact, some business books will tell you not to play favorites at work, but I play favorites, big time. Who are my favorites? The visionaries—they get all of me.

And now, what about those fence sitters? If you properly take care of your visionaries, they'll recruit your fence sitters for you. They'll sing your praises, promote your message, and support your mission to those skeptical fence sitters.

One more thing—which type are you at work: visionary, fence sitter or resister?

Does Your Culture Work?

In my company, we try to avoid categorizing something as either *good* or *bad*. Instead, we like to say that it's either *working* or *not working*. We recognize that, while other companies might have a policy or system that works for them, the same policy or system might not work for us. That doesn't make it a bad policy; it just doesn't work for us. When something works, we celebrate it. When something doesn't work, we change it.

I share this information with the challenge that you evaluate the culture and community of your workplace. Do they work? Are the staff and customers happy? Does the community around your business benefit by having you in it? And, yes, is your company making money? The company could be doing wonderful, amazing things to improve the lives of the people it employs and serves, but if it's not profitable, then it's doubtful that the company will be around much longer to continue doing amazing things.

Values and Behaviors

Whenever it starts to feel like a community is lazy or lacking the commitment necessary to cultivate and promote a healthy environment, people are tempted to "throw the baby out with the bathwater" or "reinvent the wheel" by coming up with a whole new idea or system to solve the problem. If you discover areas in which your company is not working, it might be because your behaviors aren't aligned with your values.

I can't count the number of times that a staff meeting or training has begun with a line of questioning like this: "Do you all value successful relationships? Do you all value fun and harmony? Do you all value teamwork?" Obviously the response would be, "Of course we value those things."

Getting clear about what you *value* gives you the opportunity to challenge each other and make sure that your *behavior* is in line with those values. When your behavior and values are not aligned, your self-esteem is battered and your confidence diminishes.

If you value health and wellness but eat a bad diet, smoke and drink heavily, and never exercise, what will happen to your self-esteem? It gradually fades away.

If you say you value knowledge and growth but never seek out seminars, enroll in college courses, or read books, what will happen to your sense of worth? Gone.

If you say you value relationships at work but refuse to attend staff meetings, retreats, and activities, what will happen to your confidence? It disappears like a thief in the night.

You can see how important it is to align your behaviors with your values. If you value and want to create a BE NICE community, try incorporating the following behaviors. Each is explained in the next section:

Recognize and support the whole person

Build successful relationships

Practice customer-focused leadership

Go in asking

Follow the twenty-four-hour rule

Own it

Create payday every day

Recognize and Support the Whole Person

Remember how we were taught that we should divide up our lives? We were taught, "This is your personal life, this is your physical life, over here are your relationships, and over here is your spirituality—and you should keep all of those areas separate and divided." Could you figure out how to make that happen? I know I never could. I wondered, "So in other words, I'm supposed to leave my *soul* at home when I go to work?" That never made much sense to me.

What does make sense is to *not* divide up your life. What does make sense is to take your entire, complex, beautiful self with you everywhere you go, even to work. And it also makes sense to create a culture that allows and even encourages every employee to do the same.

▣ Build Successful Relationships

I truly believe that a successful company or business is made up of successful relationships between the people who work there. You could walk into a store that has marble floors, amazing displays, award-winning imagery, and a multimillion-dollar advertising campaign, but if there are *not* successful relationships between the staff members who work there, will the customer notice? You bet. Do customers want to spend money in that type of store? Probably not.

No matter the size of the company, no matter the product or service you provide, all companies are made up of human beings who work there, and who sometimes spend more hours with co-workers than they spend with their own families. Of course you have a job to perform and tasks to execute every single day. However—and here's where businesses often go blind—to every task that must be performed, a human being is attached. I would like to propose that your relationship with those human beings is far more important than getting the task accomplished.

At one of my business locations, we have a catchall storage room commonly referred to as "the dungeon." Anything and everything can end up in the dungeon, and venturing into that room is often preceded with the announcement, "Cover me, I'm going in!"

One of our team members is a clean freak and very task-oriented. On occasion, when he was feeling extra eager, he'd attack the dungeon with a vengeance and would resurface hours later, proclaiming it clean and organized. Unfortunately, in the process of "civilizing" the dungeon, he'd exterminate relationships with his fellow workers. In the process of getting the job done, he'd accuse this co-worker of making a mess of the dungeon, annoy another person with the "drama" of cleaning, and belittle another co-worker for not offering to pitch in.

Eventually, he'd come to me with the proud announcement, "Look! The dungeon is clean," and I'd respond, "Yeah, but you left ten people in your wake. Ten people dislike you and detest their jobs. Now that the dungeon is clean, please go back and clean up your relationships."

Let me reemphasize that, for every task that must be performed, human beings are attached to those tasks. Your relationship with those human beings is far more important than getting the task accomplished.

▣ Practice Customer-Focused Leadership

When it comes to being successful in any business or industry, I think we all need to remind ourselves of how we make money. Who writes your paycheck? Who is your customer?

The only reason you exist in any business is because of your customers. The only reason you can buy the clothes you wear, live in the house you live in, take the vacations you take, send your kids to college, and drive the car you drive is because of your customer. Yet some businesses make their customers feel unwelcome. Their frontline sales people and service providers treat customers as if they were unwelcome interruptions, rolling their eyes as if to ask, "Why can't you find someone else to help you?" Why does this happen? Because, in many business organizations, the boss makes the frontline people feel as though they're interruptions in the boss's hectic, all-important day.

Owners, leaders, and managers often assume that having their name on the building or their signature on the lease makes them the most important person in the company. Although this may be difficult to read and understand, let me tell all business owners and leaders that you are the *least* significant individual in your organization.

If you make money by having happy customers who ultimately refer more customers to your business (your best form of advertising is word of mouth), then who has the most influence on whether or not your customers are happy? It's usually not the owner or the manager. It's the frontline people—the receptionists, salespeople, cashiers, tour guides, sales clerks, secretaries, table bussers, and maintenance people—simply because they're with the customers every minute of every day.

Typical pyramid-shaped organizational charts show the owner at the top of the pyramid, followed by the management team, and then the frontline staff. Who is commonly at the bottom of the pyramid, not usually by design, but by default? The customer. Yes, it's true. If your company is riddled with hierarchy—with an "all important" focus on the boss—then your customer comes last.

Let's take that pyramid and turn it upside down. Who should be at the top? The customer, followed by the frontline staff, and then the management. And who's at the bottom? The owner. This may sound harsh, but implementing this way of thinking will make any business far more successful and profitable. And isn't that why you're in business to begin with?

If you were a guest at Disneyland and you got lost, who would you ask for directions? Would you find your way to the corporate offices, find the highly paid Disney executive, and ask him or her where you should go? *No!* You'd ask the cleaning person who was sweeping up the spilled popcorn in front of Tomorrowland. Imagine if that cleaning person responded coldly with, "I don't know. Why are you asking me? That's not my job. They don't pay me enough money to know where everything is around here." I can assure you, that's *not* how a cleaning person would respond at a Disney park. Disney makes sure their front-line people keep guests happy and coming back year after year.

I once interviewed an executive at Outback Steakhouse, an organization that I'm very impressed by. I know businesses that have challenges creating a positive, dedicated, passionate frontline team in just *one* location, and I was curious as to how Outback Steakhouse creates a fun, consistent culture in 650 locations around the world. I loved the executive's answer, because he said that the leader of their organization is not a human being, which at first confused me. When I probed more, he explained that a human being couldn't be in 650 locations every single day to inspect that the culture is intact, but a vision and a standard can be in every location, twenty-four hours a day, seven days a week. He explained that the leader of their organization is the vision of a happy customer.

The executive went on to tell me that Outback Steakhouse has yet to receive a letter from a happy customer stating, "I just love Outback Steakhouse because of your executives." So, why do people love Outback Steakhouse? It's because the hosts, bartenders, servers, bussers, line cooks—and yes, even the executives—practice customer-focused leadership. Their Web site (www.OutbackSteakhouse.com) explains their philosophy this way:

> We do things differently at Outback. We even strive to make a difference in the lives of everyone involved. Treat people "Just Right," and success is sure to follow. It's a culture of respect and camaraderie that breeds enthusiasm. It starts with entertaining each customer like a guest in our home.

When a business becomes customer focused, it makes a major paradigm shift. Every decision requires an answer to the question, "How will this affect our customers?" Every system implemented demands the analysis, "Will this provide a better shopping or service experience for our customers?" Staff members in a business that practices customer-focused leadership would never pass a customer on to another staff member, as if they didn't have the time to immediately address the customer's request.

But there's another level to this way of thinking. Customer-focused business owners, directors, and leaders understand how valuable their frontline people are for establishing customer loyalty. Customer-focused business leaders never sit behind closed office doors, hiding from the day-to-day process of creating a healthy work environment. They make it their number one priority to cultivate a fun, happy workplace. They understand that their first role is to take care of the staff, to make sure the staff is happy and provided with the resources to do their jobs with enjoyment and gratification. They know that a happy staff attracts and retains happy customers.

In consulting with a business owner a few years back, I inquired as to how he spent his day. He told me that he was in his office in the back, doing paperwork most of the time. When I asked him how much time he spent with his people up front to coach, encourage, and redirect them as they service customers all day, he said, "Oh, they can come back to my office and speak with me if they ever have a problem." With that I replied, "So, the only time you spend with your people is when they have a problem? Your people could be having amazing victories every single day, and you're never a part of that experience to congratulate them and help them feel good about their investment in your customers and your company."

In their book, *In Search of Excellence,* Tom Peters and Robert Waterman popularized a concept known as MBWA. Developed in the 1970s by Hewlett-Packard, MBWA stands for Management By Wandering Around, and it's part of the legendary "HP Way." While some business leaders and managers claim that they don't have time to wander around because they're too busy doing paperwork, HP's managers would probably respond: "How do you find all that time to do paperwork? We're too busy wandering around!"

Bottom line: Happy customers come from happy employees. Happy employees come from happy managers. Happy managers come from happy owners. And happy owners must be nice.

◼ Go In Asking

"Go in asking" is a philosophy that my company learned from Gene Juarez, a genius of a businessman in Seattle, Washington. "Go in asking" is a wonderful practice that will help you build amazing teamwork, communicate properly, and build strong relationships. Here's what it means.

Oftentimes we hear secondhand or even thirdhand stories about what a team member did or said, and we instantly want to skip to judgment and tell that person how their words or actions upset us. We immediately assume that they're guilty, and we want to tell them about it.

Rather than assuming, judging, or attacking, it's much better to "go in asking." Get with that person privately, one-on-one, and ask about the situation. Don't repeat what you heard, because that only puts them on the defensive and they'll have to address what you heard rather than the real truth. Say something such as, "Would you mind sharing with me what happened the other day?" You must not have any judgment in your voice, and you must go in with total love. Your ultimate goal is to discover the truth firsthand, so the two of you can resolve the situation, learn and grow from the experience, and cultivate a better relationship.

My experience has been that, nine times out of ten, there's always another side of the story. If I fail to "go in asking," I usually end up completely offending the person by reprimanding and judging them based on wrong information, and then I have to backpedal and apologize for speaking out prior to knowing the whole story. What a mess! If only I'd gone in asking.

◼ Follow the Twenty-Four-Hour Rule

Have you noticed that most businesses are filled with a lot of very busy people? Because everyone in your organization is interconnected with each other, and because you rely so much on teamwork, it's important to respect each other's time. To build a BE NICE culture and community, follow the twenty-four-hour rule in responding to each other's e-mails, messages, and requests.

Plainly explained, the twenty-four-hour rule is good manners. It simply means that if someone calls or e-mails you requesting information or feedback, it's polite to respond within twenty-four hours. Even if you don't have the information they request, respond within twenty-four hours to inform them that you received their message and that you'll be back in touch with them at a later time.

Own It

It's amazing the excuses we can come up with as to why things aren't up to standards, why the company isn't successful, and why we have high staff turnover. I heard it once said:

> *If you're good at coming up with excuses,*
> *you'll never be good at anything else.*

In our BE NICE culture and community, we have a belief that says if you see it, you own it. For example, if you see a gum wrapper on the floor in the reception area, the fact that you saw it means you own it. And what do you do with gum wrappers? You pick them up and throw them away. It makes no difference that it's not your gum wrapper.

If you see that morale is low and people aren't being nice to each other, then *you own it.* It doesn't matter that you may not be the boss. It doesn't matter that you're not the cause of the low morale. What matters is that you own it, and there is much you could do about it. As you learned at the beginning of this chapter, leadership is everyone's responsibility.

Create Payday Every Day

Now that's a statement that should get most people's attention, because we all love payday. Unfortunately for most people, payday happens only twice a month, on the first and fifteenth. Or worse, for others payday is only once a year when they get to take that much-needed vacation.

I don't know about you, but I've always wanted payday to be every day. I want to be rewarded on a daily basis for my efforts. I want to feel that sense of accomplishment, that thrill of achievement, that feeling of being a part of something that really makes a difference.

If you're like me, let me share with you some guidelines on how you can create payday for yourself and for the people you work with on a daily basis.

First, realize that compensation doesn't just happen from the boss to the employee. Compensation can go both ways. In a BE NICE culture, staff members consider how they compensate each other, and how they compensate the boss.

Some companies figure they can put their employees through hell and misery now because the employee will retire with some cash later. That might work for some, but not for all. In fact, I believe that practice is becoming less and less acceptable. Employees want to be happy now. People want to feel useful, productive, respected, and cared about today.

When surveys have been done with employees of different corporations in different industries, and those employees were asked to rate their priorities in order of importance, income was about seventh on the list. Does that mean people don't think their income level is important? Not at all. Money is always an issue and is undeniably a legitimate currency to let people arbitrate their value to the company. However, money is not the only form of currency. Consider these other currencies:

Love

Professionalism

Respect

Teamwork

Integrity

A sense of accomplishment

A sense of being cared about

A sense of power

A sense of purpose

A sense of fun

How "rich" is your company in providing the bonus package listed above? How secure are your holdings of those types of "stocks"? Does every person in your company have the power to endorse checks written from those accounts? How much more profitable could your company be if every employee focused on compensating each other at work by abundantly offering these other types of currencies?

Principles and Practices for True Leadership

The "old school" of working with people taught leaders to dictate, control, manipulate, and police. Have you ever worked in that type of environment? How did it make you feel? Did it work? Were you happy? Were you excited about making your boss more money?

The new school of working with people advocates a different practice, one that translates into true leadership. It calls upon every person to assume the responsibility for inspiring each other. The new school is a bit radical because it may require you to adopt a different job description, which includes the following responsibilities: inspiring people, being a coach and a cheerleader, setting a good example, and empowering people.

▣ Inspire People

Honestly ask yourself this question: When you walk through the doors into your work, does your presence in the building help to inspire people, or does it poison and intimidate them? Are you the type of person who brightens up a room by leaving?

To bring inspiration means that you possess hope, happiness, and an attitude of fun, and you want others to have those things for themselves.

▣ Be a Coach and a Cheerleader

Sometimes the best support you can receive from people at work is *not* to have them lend a hand, but rather to be your coach and cheerleader. Sometimes you just need to know that someone believes in you— believes you're capable, competent, and a true contributor to the business.

In addition to the "You jumped through fire" recognition printed in the company's newsletter, a BE NICE community also promotes the little day-to-day victories privately shared between two team members. To be a coach and cheerleader requires simple words and gestures that say, "You can do it. I believe in you."

▣ Set a Good Example

"If it's to be, it's up to me." I'm not sure where that quote came from but I learned it from my mother, and I've said it to myself and to others thousands of times. It's so easy to worry about and focus on what other people need to learn: They should learn this, they should learn that. However, it's not your job to fix and change people. Your job is to fix and change yourself, so look in the mirror because that's the man or woman you can change. And making that change in yourself can be the best lesson and example so that others will want to make the change in themselves.

Who better to teach your staff about the importance of unbelievable customer service than someone who has high customer-service ratings?

Who better to teach your co-workers about the importance of team-work than someone who truly is a team player? Who better to teach your team at work about the excitement of your industry than someone who truly is excited? As the old saying goes, if you can't walk into your work or office with a smile on your face, go to bed the night before with a coat hanger in your mouth.

▣ Empower People

I love the word *empowerment.* It carries with it a feeling of hope mixed in with the idea of growth. When you empower someone, you offer them tools, resources, training, support, a little bit of guidance, and a lot of belief in their ability. You give them hope.

What a sad belief, "If you want something done right, do it your-self." When you empower people, you're doing all that you can to set them up to win. At the same time, you're allowing them to make some mistakes, just as you did when you were learning and growing.

A True Leader

Although I've stressed the point that everyone can and should be a leader in the workplace community, I can't leave this section without saying a few words about the importance of the leadership that comes from the top.

You can possess a business card that says you're the boss, or be promoted to a position that gives you control and authority over other people, but that doesn't necessarily make you a leader.

The definition of a true leader is someone who gets the job done, along with the efforts of other people who gladly and confidently follow. Notice that there are a couple of parts to that statement. I know of business leaders who get the job done along with the efforts of their people, but their people don't "gladly and confidently follow" them. In fact, a lot of bosses try to lead through fear and intimidation. To me, that's not the sign of a good leader. If you had to work for a boss like you, would you quit?

A toxic work environment is usually created at the top. Not that the newest people in a company couldn't have a major impact on creating a healthier, happier, and friendlier environment, because they can and they do. But to cultivate a culture that is nice and therefore feels good, even to customers, true leadership must come from the top.

The Boss Is in the Building

Suppose you're the boss. Even if you dug a tunnel from your house to your work, and came up through a hole in your closed and locked office, the staff would still know the boss was in the building. Why is this important to understand and accept?

We all agree that happy customers are loyal because they're serviced and taken care of by happy employees, and happy employees come from happy bosses. If you want to create a fun and happy atmosphere, which we all know will translate into more profitability, then it's *very* necessary that the mood, the feeling, and the theme for the day come from the top. As Matt Weinstein suggests in his book, *Managing to Have Fun,* if you want to offer service with a smile, make sure you give *everyone* in your company something to smile about.

Let's create a scenario to make this point. Again, let's say you're the boss, and you own a store with hundreds of employees who service thousands of customers. Let's say you come to work one day, and you happen to be in a *very* good mood, but you also happen to be very busy, with a lot on your plate. You pull into the parking lot of your store, walk into your building, pass by your hundreds of employees and customers, go straight upstairs to your office, and close the door. Now, granted, you're in a very good mood, but what will the buzz and the whispering be in your building within about five minutes? You got it: "The boss is in a bad mood. Don't go near the boss. Everyone lay low today." With that mood in your store that day, what will happen to staff morale? What will happen to creativity? What will happen to teamwork? What will happen to *profits?*

To be a true leader, you need to own not only the reality of how things are, you must also own people's perception of how things are. It's not enough for you to actually be in a good mood. A staff member could come up to my office and say, "Hey Winn, the whole company thinks you're in a bad mood." I could respond with, "Well, I'm not. I'm in a great mood. That's their problem if they think I'm in a bad mood." But where will that get me?

If people don't know you're in a good mood, or they assume you're *not* in a good mood, you still have work to do. As a leader, you must own the perception.

When I arrive at work each day, it takes me at least thirty minutes to get to my office. Why? Because I visit every square inch of my facility to show my smiling, happy face to staff and customers, and to hug as many people as I can. I visit each office, every classroom, the staff lunch room, the laundry room, the sales area . . . *everywhere*. I want people in that building to know I'm in a great mood, I love coming to work, I love my job, and I appreciate each one of them. And on those days when I don't feel that way, I fake it.

If people at work aren't nice, especially the boss, it's almost guaranteed that the staff won't be having fun. When the staff isn't having fun, they don't laugh together. And when they don't laugh together, creativity goes down and absenteeism skyrockets. It's that simple.

Having Fun (It's Not Rocket Science)

As business professionals, we constantly strive to upgrade our business expertise and fine-tune our competence. Now it's time to implement one more necessary ingredient for running a successful business:

Fun! Laughter! Make your business a party!

In some companies, if laughter rings through the office, what does that imply? *People aren't doing their job. Get back to work. No laughing around here.* Please don't think I'm getting off track and dismissing all principles of professionalism, because whether you realize it or not, I'm proclaiming increased profitability. The intentional use of fun can be a powerful force in team building, improving customer service, improving team attitude and loyalty, and ultimately increasing profitability.

As Matt Weinstein suggests in his book, *Managing to Have Fun*, if several other businesses in your area offer a wonderful customer experience, your customers have a choice about where to spend their money. Of course they're going to make a decision with their heads, but they're also going to spend money with their gut. They're going to ask themselves, "How do I feel about spending time in your place of business? Do I like you? Do I trust you? Are you nice?"

Do businesses where staff members have fun, like each other, and treat customers as if they're happy to be there have a competitive advantage? Absolutely. Those businesses leave their clients feeling good about spending money there. As *Managing to Have Fun* emphasizes, if you want to offer service with a smile, make sure you give the people you work with something to smile about. Studies show that when staff members laugh together, creativity and production go up and absenteeism goes down. A staff that laughs together stays together.

You can create an environment of fun, laughter, and enthusiasm in your business by making fun a daily priority, not an occasional event. Creating an environment of enthusiasm doesn't mean, "We'll have fun a week from Sunday at that company picnic we have planned." Having fun at work is a day-to-day attitude.

Don't assume that you and your team will occasionally laugh together, and don't wait for it to happen. All companies must create experiences and events where people can have fun and laugh with each other, and the following ideas can help you do this.

Please note that these ideas are not an all-or-nothing philosophy. You have the option to implement all of these ideas or none of them, depending on the size of your organization, the constraints of your product or service, your safety regulations, or the nature of the business. Just remember that while you're trying to create fun at work, you're also respecting the company's guidelines and standards. So, within that framework, here are some ideas to help you make sure that fun happens, and that it happens often.

▣ Create Simple, Silly Rituals and Activities

In Oprah Winfrey's wonderful *O* magazine, there was an article titled "Spa Girls." In it, Oprah shared her story about a small group of her friends who vowed and even contracted with each other to become healthy and fit together.

As a team in my company, we decided to follow Oprah's example by initiating a simple gesture of teamwork toward a common goal of wellness. We started the Eight Glasses of Water Club.

It was quite simple. All of our staff members received their own plastic water bottles, on which they wrote their names using a big permanent marker. Each twelve-ounce water bottle represented two glasses of water, which meant it had to be emptied four times a day. Here's where it got fun. Each time someone emptied their bottle, they had to have another team member autograph it, with the goal of four different signatures by the end of the day.

Sound simple and childish? Ask my staff—they think it's a hoot. It forced some of the more shy-type team members to come out of their shells a bit to intermingle. It created dialogues with our customers about health and fun. It opened up more opportunities for the staff to focus on health and wellness, but more important, to do it as a team.

One final note. After downing about four or five glasses of water, the Eight Glasses of Water Club soon turned into the Mad Dash to the Restroom Club.

▣ Play Loud, Fun, Party Music

Another easy way to have fun at work is to play loud, fun, party music in your store or office as the staff arrives each morning. Upbeat party music may not be suitable for your ambiance during business hours (we change ours to light jazz when the clients begin to arrive), but how about throwing a party every morning as the staff begins to arrive? You can get them off to a fun, happy start by playing the theme from *Rocky*, or "YMCA." Get the boss dancing to that one, and let the party begin!

A successful businessman visited one of my facilities years ago and experienced the energy that the fun music created for our students and staff. Later, he told me that when he left, he immediately called his own managers to request they do the same.

▣ Have Theme Days

Still another idea for bringing more fun to your workplace is to have theme days where the entire staff dresses alike or shares some common goal or focus for having a fun, enthusiastic day. Although we've been doing this in my company for years, more recently we've assigned different committees to make a consistent day each month a theme day.

Theme days could include Prom Friday, where everyone dresses in their high school–era prom attire and/or brings in their prom pictures for a good laugh.

Your company could host Beach Day, Country-Western Day, '60s Day, Hippie Day, Pajama Day, or Rock Star Day. To really make your theme day fun and effective, find out what would be fun for your team. How do you find out? You ask them.

Please note that you will always want to include your customers and clients as part of the fun. You never want to make the client feel excluded, left in the dark, or taking a back seat to your theme day.

▣ Create Traditions as a Team

Traditions can take any form or shape. Just to give you some examples, in my company we've traveled together to Hawaii, Europe, Mexico, and to see Broadway shows in New York City.

We've had overnight parties in a mountain cabin, played together at water parks, and hosted a '70s disco roller-skating party.

We've read books together, such as *The One Minute Manager, Raving Fans, The Greatest Salesman in the World, Flight of the Buffalo, You Can Heal Your Life*, and many others.

Together we've attended weddings, gotten tattoos, cried at funerals, danced at concerts, and learned at seminars.

We have company traditions such as The Caper, when our students and staff earn their way to attend a pleasurable three-day educational event in a fun city such as Las Vegas. We stay at a great hotel, host a big dinner party, see shows, have two full days of fun, and then attend a full day of education.

We've had our company logo printed on T-shirts, umbrellas, beach towels, watches, hats, jewelry, Tiffany key rings, and my staff's favorite—jogging outfits.

We've done all this while at the same time improving our customer service policies, creating a better experience for our staff and customers, getting married, buying homes, raising children, and earning more money.

Years ago, we made it a tradition to *not* invite spouses to any of our company events—not even to our December holiday party. For some reason, we all feel like we can be ourselves if we don't have to wonder whether or not our spouse, significant other, or date is having a good time. I would never say that's how it should be for other companies and organizations; I'm just sharing what we decided as a team. Once again, how do you know what will work best for your team? You ask them, which makes everyone feel important, included, and supported as people.

▣ ▣ ▣

This chapter covered a lot of material on the subject of being nice at work. You might be wondering, "Winn, what about those staff members who don't want to participate? What about those staff members who refuse to attend staff meetings, or who refuse to add anything positive, fun, or uplifting to the staff? What should we do with them?"

My answer? SW, SW, SW! Remember, it stands for:

Some will, some won't, so what!

In time, people will either get it or they won't. Either they'll stick around and become amazing team members, or they'll move on. But the lesson for you, my friend, is not to waste too much energy there. Remember, you've got the *new* mind-set to find those staff members who will want to play with you. Some will. Some will. Some will. Find them.

Your Home-Play Assignment:

What If None of This Comes from the Top?

Many times after I've shared this information in a seminar or workshop, a group of excited yet disillusioned people have come up to me and said something like, "Our boss should have been here. He's the real problem. What if we all want to be nice, but our boss is an SOB?"

All I can say is that my heart goes out to you. To pay the bills, you sometimes have to endure unpleasantness at work. But I challenge you to try the following home-play assignment:

1. Discover bits and pieces of ideas I've shared here that you could subtly or even privately implement at work, without going against company policies.

2. Perhaps you can share one or two ideas with a co-worker.

People love to commiserate against the boss in a negative way, and I doubt that your workplace allows that. Why not be a new type of rebel—one who has the courage to not only inspire the naysayer at work, but to also take on the challenge of inspiring the big, bad boss?

Create, Train, and Sustain a BE NICE Community in Your Workplace

"If you want to be successful, look around to see what everyone else is doing, and then do something different."
—Walt Disney

I n the last chapter, we defined the behaviors for making BE NICE a part of your workplace culture and community. We could fundamentally agree that those behaviors are merely the "be" part of BE NICE, but now it's time to concentrate on the "do" part.

This chapter is about taking action to dramatically overhaul the way you do business—the way in which your workplace community plays and thrives in your bigger community. That overhaul process is divided into three stages: Create, train, and sustain.

Stage 1: CREATE

Because people spend a great amount of their time and energy at work, they long to belong to a company that makes them feel better about themselves and makes them feel that they do more than just earn a paycheck—they want to feel like they have a purpose and make a difference. In addition to the lives they have at home and in their churches and communities, people want to feel and believe that they belong to a community at work. Although they may come from different backgrounds, beliefs, and lifestyles, when they come to work they must all believe in the same thing and strive for the same purpose and goals—and they do that together, with a group of co-workers, eight hours a day, forty hours a week. Employees don't just work for a company, they *join* a company. Customers don't just spend money with a company, they *join* a company.

One example of this would be a company such as Harley Davidson. Customers don't just buy Harley Davidson's motorcycles, they *join* Harley Davidson. They buy the logo wear and some even have the logo tattooed on their bodies. For many, Harley Davidson has become a way of life, a sort of church, a community to belong to.

How many would agree that Disney has a culture? To define Disney's culture, you'd probably use adjectives like magical, fun, animated, happy, clean, and even expensive. If you own *any* type of business, producing *any* type of product or service, how would you enjoy having your employees and your customers define your product and service by using adjectives like those?

More than fifty thousand employees work for Disney. Do you think Disney was able to find fifty thousand people who naturally had the skills and know-how to create a magical, fun, animated, happy, and clean experience for their guests? Hardly. In fact, according to John DiJulius, a good friend and admired businessman who has studied successful businesses for his book *Secret Service,* perhaps only 5 percent of the people in our society naturally possess those skills. Disney *created* a culture, and then they *trained* people within their culture to provide the magical, fun, animated, happy, clean experience that Disney guests have come to expect and want to be a part of. People want to belong to Disney, be included in the Disney family, and feel that a Disney park is "home."

Systems, Systems, Systems

Whether you visit a Disney park in Anaheim or Tokyo, you can count on enjoying the same great experience. Whether you buy a McDonald's hamburger on the East Coast or the West Coast, you know you'll be getting the same hamburger. Why? Because successful companies like these have systems for how they do business.

Successful companies need systems for everything, but they especially need systems to create, train, and sustain a BE NICE culture and community. A *system* is loosely defined as "this is how we do things around here."

Personal interpretation cannot enter a system. If you were hired to be in the Disneyland parade, you couldn't show up with your own version of Mickey Mouse. If you're a cook at McDonald's, you can't show up with your own recipe for making a hamburger. If you work for companies like these, you join their culture and you follow their systems.

There are two qualities of a system: It's written down and it's repeated continually.

▣ A System Is Written Down

Everything about your company, whether it's a belief system, an all-important job position, or a menial task, must be written down. If it's *not* written down, it's not part of your system and therefore not part of your culture—and people can't be held responsible for or accountable to something that's not in black and white.

If your top receptionist is the only person who knows how to run the reception desk in your business, what happens to the front desk if that person goes on vacation for two weeks? It falls apart. That's not a system. It must be written down.

If you have twenty staff members working in your business, your goal should be that you could lose all twenty of those people, bring in twenty new people, and your business wouldn't skip a beat. Why? Because you'd have a written-down system for everyone to follow. They'd know exactly what to do.

▣ A System Is Repeated Continually

On occasion, a business owner will call me on the phone to say, "Winn, we took your advice and created a new system for our employee dress code. Winn, it was written down. We held a staff meeting and discussed the new dress code point by point. Every staff member was there. They all agreed to everything. But then today, half of the staff showed up dressed inappropriately. What do I do with these people?"

In response, I ask, "Have you ever trained a dog? If so, how many times do you have to say SIT?"

SIT! SIT! SIT!

You say it over and over again. The same is true for staff members who support your company culture and protect your company community.

Repetition of the beliefs and systems—SIT, SIT, SIT!—is what will train and sustain your BE NICE culture.

> *"Here are the exact words you will use to properly handle a complaining customer"* — *SIT, SIT, SIT!*

> *"This is how you answer the phone"* — *SIT, SIT, SIT!*

> *"This is how you offer the customer a cup of coffee"* — *SIT, SIT, SIT!*

> *"This is what you need to wear to work"* — *SIT, SIT, SIT!*

If you haven't created a workplace culture for people to read, study, adopt, learn, and belong to, then what you have is a bunch of people showing up for one thing, and one thing only: a paycheck.

I'm guessing that your company culture already has systems for payroll, janitorial services, inventory control, and so on. However, does your culture include systems for how to get along, how to complain and communicate with each other, how to show appreciation to your co-workers, how to have fun, or how to give love and support to an employee who's in a bad marriage? Are these life experiences and basic human needs included in your policies and procedures manual? Yes, our goal is to keep things professional at work, but human emotions and life experiences will come up.

Prior to creating a culture in my company—which meant that all systems and beliefs had to be written down and discussed over and over again—we had hundreds of infractions every single day and never knew about them. We had insubordination, we had people subtly but perhaps not consciously sabotaging someone else's career, we had demoralizing comments regarding co-workers—and we never knew about these infractions. We never knew that our culture was under attack, simply because we didn't know what our culture was. How was our culture defined? What did we believe in? What was our purpose together outside of making the cash register ring? All we knew was that it oftentimes wasn't fun at work, that we had high staff turnover, that we were attracting the wrong people, and that decent individuals were having a difficult time supporting and loving each other.

Today in our company, with hundreds of people working with us, one person could slip up, speak inappropriately, or do something that doesn't contribute to who we are, and a hundred co-workers would immediately recognize the infraction and kick into high gear to coach, redirect, support, and cheerlead that person into adhering to the beliefs of the culture. If someone has sworn their life to negativity and refuses to learn or adopt the behaviors and practices of our community, that person is usually immediately rejected—they either quit (it's difficult to be a dysfunctional warrior on your own), or they're "NEXT-ed."

NEXT-ing People

Some companies fire people. We call it NEXT-ing. We believe in unconditional love, but we do *not* believe in unconditional employment.

Once you've involved every staff member in creating a quality work environment, defining what being a team player really means, and teaching them what being nice and unbelievable customer service are all about—once you've properly communicated all of these company standards, you then sit down with those people and say, "We're about creating a team where coming to work every day is like group therapy. We're about creating an environment where our customers come to bask in the fun, the love, and the professionalism. We're about supporting each other in achieving balance and happiness, not just financially, but in every aspect of our lives. We're a team that's dedicated to creating all of these things. And if you don't want to play with us—NEXT!"

I remember years ago, whenever someone asked me what I looked for in hiring someone for my company, I'd ramble this big, long list: They need *this* much experience, *this* type of education, and *these* degrees. Now I just say that I want people who are nice and who have desire. I've hired people with amazing resumes, amazing education, and amazing experience, but if they were a bit mean-spirited or bitter, I couldn't work with them. Not only did I not want to be around that type of person, I also wasn't willing to expose the rest of my staff to that mean, bitter person for eight hours a day.

As I shared previously, you'll attract positive employees to your company and business by building an environment and culture that acknowledges, supports, appreciates, develops, and retains that type of person. *Build it and they will come.* A company that does not *build it* will eventually lose wonderful, positive employees.

Years ago we had a woman working for us who seemed as though she'd been weaned on a pickle. You know the type—sour, bitter, mean;

the type of person who quit your company two years ago, but just hasn't left yet. I used to think it was my job, as a business owner and leader, to fix and change my people. I have since learned that in business, *and* in personal relationships, it is *not* my job to fix and change others. But back then I thought it was, so I plotted and pleaded and begged and schemed to fix this bitter woman. Five years later, she was still the same. What did I finally do? I fired her. Yep. I finally did it. I NEXT-ed her.

Within two months of me firing this sour lady, three phenomenal, talented, hardworking, passionate individuals came knocking on my door, looking for a job. My response to them was almost, "Where were you three years ago?" But, you see, I had not *built* an environment that would attract talented, hardworking, passionate people. I had built an environment where a mean, nasty, bitter woman could stay employed for five years. Let me ask you something: Was I really doing that nasty woman a favor by allowing her to stay in my company? No way. And the minute I NEXT-ed her, we were able to attract wonderful people.

Golden Rules for Creating a BE NICE Culture

I'd like to share with you the written-down and repeated culture—the "Golden Rules" belief system—that we have created for my company. This code of conduct is who we are together as a team. It's what we all believe in, what we strive for. We truly believe that our Golden Rules will not only help us to become a more interconnected team, they'll also allow us to duplicate our culture and community over and over again, in business locations with individuals whom we may never meet. Those individuals will be able to adopt the same BE NICE philosophies and practices, and thereby duplicate the same culture and community that we live in and enjoy. Let me also add here that no rules for success will work if you don't.

Our Golden Rules contain elements that may seem ridiculously simple, but remember, if a system is not written down and repeated continually, then it's *not* part of your culture. You can't expect the people in your company's community to live by an assumed standard.

Here's our code of conduct, which we've blown up poster size and hung in every location so that our hundreds of employees can see it every day. In the pages that follow, I'll expand on each of these rules.

The Golden Rules for a BE NICE Culture

1. Always be on time.

2. Always be in a great mood (fake it when necessary).

3. Come to work prepared.

4. Be informed (read all memos and information).

5. Gossip is not allowed.

6. Hold each other accountable (use the twenty-four-hour rule).

7. Resolve all personal challenges with love.

8. Go to the decision maker with any apparently unsolvable challenges.

9. Be knowledgeable, literate, and articulate.

10. Always "look the part" of an impeccable professional.

11. Be professional always.

12. Do not get personally involved with clients.

13. Personal lives remain personal.

1. Always Be on Time

Spell out for everyone in your company exactly what "being on time" looks like. For example, if your work is some type of store that opens its doors at 9 A.M., then one of your employees could rush in promptly at 9 A.M. and claim to be on time. But what if customers also arrive at 9 A.M. and therefore have to be exposed to a frazzled, rushed employee? Perhaps showing up to work at 9 A.M. for a 9-to-5 shift would not be "on time." Define what being on time looks like in your company, and be very specific.

2. Always Be in a Great Mood (Fake It When Necessary)

A very good friend of mine, Eric Fisher, owns a successful business in Wichita, Kansas. Eric says he has two reasons for firing an employee from his company: if they steal from him, and if they show up to work in a bad mood. If someone comes to work in a bad mood, he'll fire them on the spot. But he'll rehire them five minutes later if they leave and come back in a good mood.

I'd like to propose that on the day we all decided to enter the work-force and take on a job with any company, we gave up the right to ever come to work in a bad mood.

There are days when you leave work and your reservoir (all those things that make you wonderful) is drained, it's empty. Good for you. Congratulations. That's supposed to happen, because that means you gave everything you had to your customers that day, or you put every-thing into your co-workers that day. But maybe you go home and you don't fill your reservoir back up, which means you're now tempted to come into work the next day in a bad mood. What do you do on those days? You *fake it.* You sit in your car in the parking lot for an extra five minutes, crank that music to cheer yourself up, and talk yourself out of that bad mood. When you walk through those doors, it's show time. And you gave up the right to be in a bad mood.

I once was in one of my business locations and asked an employee, "Hey, how are you today?" She theatrically threw her arms up in the air and whisked past me while convincingly proclaiming, "I'm faking it!" All day long nobody had any idea that she was *not* having a good day.

3. Come to Work Prepared

Coming to work prepared means that you're ready and available to work as effectively as possible—whatever that may look like. Perhaps it means you eat a great breakfast and do yoga before work so your mind is clear and ready to focus. Perhaps it means you lay out your clothes the night before, so your image matches the product you represent. Or maybe you arrive early enough to unclutter your workspace and start the day fresh.

I enthusiastically believe in karma—what goes around, comes around. What you put out to the universe is what you get back. We all want to make more money (I believe that those who say they don't want to make more money would lie about other things as well), so it serves us to give more of ourselves at work than we're paid to give. When you give more, you eventually get paid accordingly. If you're being paid fifteen dollars per hour, then work as though you were being paid twenty dollars per hour, and eventually that commitment will be rewarded.

4. Be Informed (Read All Memos and Information)

We used to have a disorder in my company that we called the "But I didn't know" syndrome. People would fall into that pattern often: *But I didn't know we had an early staff meeting Tuesday morning. But I didn't know I had to fill out that paperwork. But I didn't know that was the company dress code.*

If you were pulled over by a police officer for speeding, would it be an acceptable defense to say, "But I didn't know the speed limit was only twenty-five miles per hour"? Ignorance is not an acceptable defense for breaking the law, and it can't be an acceptable defense in your BE NICE culture. Let people know that it's their job to know. It's everyone's job to *know* your culture, to *know* what's expected of them, to *know* your company's mission statement, to *know* your policies and procedures, and to *know* what's happening and when.

5. Gossip Is Not Allowed

I doubt that too many people would argue the fact that gossip is a serious cancer in a company. Gossip has many faces, and it can destroy a community. It's a sneaky, clever, subtle, and unnatural side of human nature—and you'll want to proactively recognize when gossip exists and have the courage to do whatever it takes to eliminate it from your company.

Easily identifiable, gossip can be defined as anything said that is not supportive or uplifting for the individual being talked about.

6. Hold Each Other Accountable (Use the Twenty-Four-Hour Rule)

As I shared previously, it's vital for a company or business to adopt a culture and belief system that encourages positive reinforcement of employee performance, commitment, and attitudes. This is done by adopting the new job description of being a coach and a cheerleader for each other. Although perfection can never be achieved (there's always room for improvement of your company's product and performance), your goal should be *excellence.* Excellence carries with it the drive and the hope for constant improvement.

But let's face it—you're going to screw up on occasion, and you therefore need a system to keep your BE NICE culture intact. How do you do that? You hold each other accountable. However, the manner in which you hold each other accountable can make or break the culture.

First, the accountability session must take place within twenty-four hours of the infraction. (Like other forms of communication, accountability should follow the twenty-four-hour rule described in chapter 8.) Second, *all* infractions are shared privately, behind closed doors. And finally, the intent and motive behind the process of holding each other accountable is that everyone grows and that everyone is accountable for the overall success of the company.

7. Resolve All Personal Challenges with Love

In high school, if we had a problem with someone, we'd tell four other people about it, so that by the time we actually voiced it to the person, we had "ammo" to state our case: *I think you're horrible, and they all agree with me!* This Golden Rule is appropriate, valid, and necessary to help you unlearn that method and, instead, resolve issues and grievances with love.

First, anytime you have a grievance with someone, make sure that you keep private both what the person did or said to upset you, and the action you take to resolve it. It's a wonderful practice to praise people publicly, and to reprimand privately.

Second, as Steven Covey, the brilliant author of *Seven Habits of Highly Effective People,* writes, begin with the end in mind. If you want the ending of your problem-resolution session to be a screaming match and to destroy your relationship with that person, then by all means go in attacking, accusing, blaming, and screaming. But if the end you have in mind is to resolve the challenge in order for the two of you to move forward without repeating the mistake—to not only maintain a constructive and positive relationship with that person, but to also cultivate more respect and teamwork between the two of you— then rehearse that type of outcome in your mind, so you'll choose to resolve the challenge with love.

Let me add here that not only does the "sender" need to share the information with love; the "receiver" must also approach the situation with love.

8. Go to the Decision Maker with Any Apparently Unsolvable Challenges

Why is it that when a person has a problem at work, they tell everyone but the person who could actually do something about it? Why waste your "woe is me" dribble on someone who can do nothing to resolve your challenge? Respect your company's line of authority and systems for communication, decide who the decision maker is, and take your challenge directly to that person. To take it to anyone else is gossip, plain and simple.

9. Be Knowledgeable, Literate, and Articulate

This Golden Rule is pretty straightforward. It doesn't say, "*Hope to be* knowledgeable, literate, and articulate." It simply challenges employees, owners, and new hirees to *be* those things.

I'd like to challenge companies, stores, and businesses to take this to another level, where everyone understands that theirs is a self-managed career. That means taking responsibility for your education, your knowledge, and your growth, rather than expecting or assuming that the company should provide all the education.

10. Always "Look the Part" of an Impeccable Professional

Whatever your business, you'll want to dress, act, and look the part of the type of business you represent. (Would you trust a dentist who didn't have any teeth?) In fact, you'll want to look the part of the most successful person with your same job.

If your job requires you to wear a uniform, this still applies. Why is it that one person wearing a uniform can look awful, disheveled, and unprofessional, while another person with the same uniform looks amazing?

Bottom line, it's a good idea to dress beyond where you are in life and to look as though you're more successful than you really are. Why? Because people don't like to give money to people who look like they don't have any money.

> *But I can't afford to wear expensive clothes. They don't pay me the salary of an executive, so why do I have to dress like one?*

Excuses, excuses, excuses. You don't need to spend a lot of money to look the part of an impeccable professional. Perhaps if you dressed like an executive now, you might be looked upon as executive material.

Whenever I discuss this topic with an audience, I always ask for a show of hands of those who take pride in being able to look *amazing* without spending a lot of money, and hundreds of hands go up. Find those talented people and ask them to take you shopping. Your closet may be filled with mistakes, but vintage stores are full of discoveries.

11. Be Professional Always

The opposite of professional is *amateur*. Which would you prefer to be dubbed? Customers don't decipher an employee's status in the company before deciding whether or not they're impressed or unimpressed. There could be a thousand people working for a company, but if the minimum-paid receptionist is cold, rude, and unprofessional when he or she answers the phone, the customer's perception of the entire company and its employee base is that *everyone* is cold, rude, and unprofessional.

Every person working for a company has an impact—either positive or negative—on the customer's experience. Every individual should be professional always, because whether you realize it or not, customers are watching and judging.

12. Do Not Get Personally Involved with Clients

All businesses are for profit, and continued profit is derived from having clients and customers who continue to spend money with your company. Whenever an employee or representative of your company gets personally involved with clients (in a dating situation, for example), you run the risk of messing with continued loyalty from that customer. To put it bluntly, my advice is *Don't s--- where you eat!*

13. Personal Lives Remain Personal

Although the strength of your company community is based on the consistency of the culture you collectively believe in, people do have separate and private lives outside of work. Although curious, "inquiring minds" want to know the personal details of co-workers and clients, divulging such information could offend the person and destroy your culture and community. Therefore, personal lives must remain personal. Unless a person wants to share the intimacies of their personal life in order to receive support and advice, it's no one's business to know whether or not so-and-so is divorced, gay, straight, a recovering addict, or any other personal, private detail.

Stage 2: TRAIN

I'm told there are studies (don't ask me where these studies are) showing that the reason people leave an organization or company is because they get bored. When people are bored, they get burned out.

Burnout is not necessarily due to a person's workload. I know people who lie on the coach all day doing nothing, and they're burned out.

The best solution for burnout is education, which is one of the best employee benefits a company can offer. Although Golden Rule number nine challenges individuals to take responsibility for their own education, staff loyalty is greatly enhanced when a company assumes a lot of the responsibility for providing education and growth opportunities for its people. And when a staff sticks around, so do the customers.

> *"If you think education is expensive, try ignorance!"*
>
> —Vidal Sassoon

I'm not referring to one educational event per year. Training needs to be ongoing. You can't provide just one seminar on teamwork and expect teamwork to flourish. That would be like attending only one aerobics class and proclaiming, "I'm fit for life." As motivational speaker Tony Robbins says, you'd never think to leave the house in the morning without brushing your teeth, even though you brushed your teeth yesterday.

You and your people need to train, train, train—SIT, SIT, SIT! In my company, we provide our people with a minimum of sixteen hours of training every single month. That training doesn't always have to be about your industry, your product, your service, or your customer service policies. The training you provide could be on topics such as these:

Improving your relationship at home

Balancing your money and getting out of debt

CPR or first aid

Fundamentals of investing in the stock market

Yoga, tai chi, or some other type of exercise

Transcendental meditation

Feng shui for the home or office

A book discussion group

A pastries cooking course

Learning a second language

Improving your creative and professional writing skills

Won't or Can't?

I learned years ago to evaluate *why* people weren't doing their jobs, and to recognize whether it's because they *won't* or they *can't*. When they won't do their job, it means there's an attitude challenge, but using the brilliant culture training described in this book can inspire people to feel good about themselves and therefore want to do their jobs. When they can't do their job, it means they need more training, more information, more resources, and more guidance—in other words, more education. Education keeps you and your people growing, and it keeps your company flourishing.

Developing Effective Training

Just because "education" is happening doesn't necessarily mean that learning is taking place. There can be many blocks and barriers to effective training. For example, researchers now know that there are many different types of learners, yet a lot of educational programs speak to only one type of learner. With a staff of twenty attending a company educational event, perhaps only four or five are actually learning.

Another barrier to effective training is fear. There can be so much fear revolving around education, and that fear can prevent learning. Fear can be the result of old, traditional educational experiences. Perhaps a grade school teacher told you many years ago that you were a bad reader, or maybe you were made to feel stupid for asking a question in a high school class, and those experiences created barriers of fear that keep you from learning effectively today.

Education can be quite expensive, and for some companies the money they spend to educate their people is like throwing pasta at the wall—sometimes it sticks and sometimes it doesn't. Education has one purpose: to change behavior. If, after a training session, nothing new is implemented and nothing changes, then the education and the money were wasted.

To properly train people within your company culture requires removing any blocks or fears and making education a fun experience. To do that in my company, we've developed some principles for creating the ultimate learning experience. Once again, these principles have been made into posters, and they hang in every company location for all to read, study, believe in, and follow.

Guiding Principles for the Ultimate Learning Experience

1. Education is an adventure of discovery.

2. People learn best when they're having fun.

3. Making a mistake isn't fatal. We make "discoveries," not "mistakes."

4. Learning is blocked when fear is present.

5. Praise is the best motivator.

6. The learning process isn't good or bad; it's simply working or not working. If it's working, we improve it. If it's not working, we change it.

7. The word *education* means "to draw out," not "to put in."

8. Learning opportunities are everywhere.

9. The goal of education is to inspire change in beliefs and behavior.

10. A staff that trains together stays together.

1. Education Is an Adventure of Discovery

This just sounds so right. Rather than education being a "do we have to go?" experience in your company, spell it out right up front that education is meant to be an adventure.

2. People Learn Best When They're Having Fun

As I said earlier, if I'm not having fun with something, I won't do it for very long. I assume that a lot of people are like me, so I want to make education fun. If education is a chore, are you going to stick with it for very long?

There's nothing more amazing and inspiring than a group of grown adults who are "playing" as though they were children—all barriers, judgments, and fears are let go, and their lighthearted, resourceful selves are allowed to create and just be. A company or business that not only promotes but also facilitates that process will undoubtedly cultivate staff loyalty, which no competitor could touch.

3. Making a Mistake Isn't Fatal. We Make "Discoveries," Not "Mistakes"

I love this one, because many of us were punished or shamed for making what was categorized as a mistake while we tried to learn.

I was at an esthetic school one day and saw a student wax off a client's entire eyebrow. The instructor who witnessed it turned to the student and said, "Wow, what an amazing discovery you just made!" Will the student ever do that again? Nope. And why was it a positive learning experience and discovery for the student—one from which she could learn, rather than a mistake that would only create more negative blocks? Because she wasn't traumatized by the learning leader. There was no pain attached to the experience, and she was therefore able to learn and move on.

4. Learning Is Blocked When Fear Is Present

Fear has many faces, and they all block the learning process. Fear comes up as boredom, ego, resistance, disruptiveness, unresponsiveness, or any other self-defeating action. Simply stated, the exact opposite of fear is *joy*. Turn education into a joyful experience, and people are freed to let go of their resistance and fear.

To create joy, rather than telling people that they should or should not learn something, challenge them to "try on" a new idea or practice. When you go shopping, you *try on clothes*. You haven't bought them yet; you're just trying them on—no commitment until you feel comfortable. The same process of trying on new ideas allows people to venture outside of their limiting comfort zones. The script here would be as basic and nonthreatening as, "Try on this new system for how we service our customer. How does that feel? How would it make our customer feel if we treated them that way? How could this benefit our store's reputation and increase profits?"

Another way to create joy and remove fear in an educational environment is to help the participants focus on the benefits of the learning experience. Ask each attendee to answer this question: *What was the BEST idea you learned from this learning experience for making you more successful?*

5. Praise Is the Best Motivator

It's a basic human need to receive recognition and praise. I believe it's a stronger motivator than money, and that people will work harder for praises than for raises.

Praise must be genuine, and it must be worthwhile—meaning you wouldn't want to dish out praises without merit. Praise must also be specific. To tell someone they're really "cool" may not do the trick, unless you're specific about why they're cool. Use a script such as, "I think it was amazing how you went out of your way to defuse that frustrated customer. I loved how you kept your cool, spoke softly to her, and smiled the entire time she was venting to you. It was very obvious to me and to the customer that you were truly listening to her complaint with compassion."

6. The Learning Process Isn't Good or Bad; It's Simply Working or Not Working. If It's Working, We Improve It. If It's Not Working, We Change It.

Language and the words we use are so important, especially during the learning process. If you remove limiting judgments and dialogue as they relate to education, you'll increase the positive effects of the training offered. Avoid using adjectives such as *good, bad, right,* or *wrong.*

7. The Word *Education* Means "to Draw Out," Not "to Put In"

We've all had a teacher or professor who was just a "talking head," reading from a boring textbook, attempting to dump information into his or her students.

In my schools, we no longer use the titles "teachers" or "instructors." Instead, we use "learning leaders" because their job is to facilitate the process of learning.

When learning leaders believe that their learners (students) are already smart, capable, and creative beings—and that their job is to facilitate a fun, adventurous, educational experience—then the God-given potential and brilliance that lies in each learner can naturally flow and develop.

8. Learning Opportunities Are Everywhere

I love telling people that thirty things happened to them today before they even arrived at work, and that every one of those things can be learning opportunities.

Education doesn't just happen in a classroom setting. In fact, without these Guiding Principles, education will surely *not* happen in a classroom. When you believe and practice what it takes to remove the fear revolving around education, then you're set free to discover learning opportunities everywhere.

9. The Goal of Education Is to Inspire Change in Beliefs and Behavior

Again, without guidance and permission to implement what you learn in educational events, the education is wasted. Know that following an educational event you want things to be done differently the very next day. Don't hide your implementation of the new information and education you receive—let everyone see you "trying things on" and doing things differently.

10. A Staff That Trains Together, Stays Together

Proper training inspires growth and maturity. There seems to be a bonding "I want to support and protect you" type experience between staff members when they go through training and growth together.

The U.S. Army knows that camaraderie between troops will only make for a stronger force of protection against its enemies. Not that businesses have enemies, but they do have competitors, and what better way to have the competitive edge than to bring a team together often to learn and grow collectively?

Stage 3: SUSTAIN

The process of sustaining a BE NICE culture and community is where the real work begins. In fact, I believe that perhaps 25 percent of your time, energy, and focus will be in the create and train stages, but 75 percent of your time, energy, and focus will be in the sustain stage.

Sustaining a culture is mostly about proper communication. Communication has all sorts of faces and vehicles. If you think posted memos or e-mails make for sufficient communication, you'll beat your head against the water cooler for the next ten years, wondering why the brilliant ideas you created have gone by the wayside and why you're still dealing with the same old problems.

I truly believe that whenever there's a problem or challenge in a company, it's because relationships between staff members have broken down. And I believe that relationships break down because of a lack of communication—end of story. It's not as if the relationship between two co-workers breaks down because one of them suddenly decides to become a jerk. Their relationship breaks down because they stop communicating.

Effective communication needs to be varied, consistent, positive, productive, fun, and constant. Communication can and does look like this:

Staff meetings

Theme Fridays

Staff celebrations

Volunteering or serving the community together

Staff retreats

One-on-one evaluations

Award ceremonies

Do we use e-mail and memos in my company? Big time. Do we think that e-mail will sustain our culture and community? Hardly.

Working or Not Working

Sometimes when we have negative challenges or downswings in our relationships, we're tempted to call it something other than what it is. We can have a mishap in our communication with a person at work, and we want to react by making a proclamation, such as, "That person is bad." We're tempted to throw the baby out with the bathwater—we want to throw a good relationship out because a bad thing happened.

To repeat something I shared previously, in my company we've learned to change our language and dialogue. Instead of stating that something is either "good" or "bad," we say it's either "working" or "not working." When something is working, such as a relationship, we celebrate it. When something is not working, we change it. Changing a relationship that's not working can sometimes be as simple as improving communication, which we often accomplish in our staff meetings.

Staff Meetings = Staff Communication

If you think about it, you might have more of a "marriage" going on at work than at your own home—you might spend more time with people at work than you do with your own spouse and family. That's why relationships in your workplace community are so important.

I want to keep emphasizing that anytime there's a problem or challenge at work, it's because relationships between staff members have broken down. And relationships break down because of a lack of communication. Staff meetings are all about communication.

In my company, we don't mind telling people that we're a "house of meetings." Why? Because we value relationships, and we make sure that our behavior is in line with what we value. The behavior to sustain healthy, successful relationships is proper and consistent communication—hence, lots and lots of meetings.

In each of my businesses, the staff participates in a daily staff meeting, which we've named Pow-Wow. It lasts for twenty minutes, and we're very specific about what we discuss and what we don't. In those twenty minutes, the staff chats about numbers, sales totals, and financial goals for the day; they choose a customer theme and focus; they plan how they're going to have fun that day; and they always end the Pow-Wow with some type of energizer, such as a cheer, a song, or an inspirational message.

The leaders of our different departments participate in a weekly management meeting. They talk about sensitive subject matters that might not be for everyone's ears, such as personnel issues or financial concerns. They also discuss the morale of the people in their departments, with an emphasis on what they're doing and what they can do to improve the well-being and growth of those they're responsible for.

Because our company is growing and our staff numbers are increasing, it's difficult for all of us to get together often, except for once a month in our Town Hall meeting. No one is eliminated from this meeting; we want everyone there. This gathering lets us reconnect with each other, it brings everyone current with the happenings of the company, and we have fun and celebrate. We look for any reason and excuse to celebrate, including birthdays, anniversaries, new staff members who've joined us, strides in the company's growth, and awards or recognition that the company has received. Bottom line, we use our Town Hall meetings to celebrate who we are and acknowledge everyone's contributions.

It is monumentally important that your staff meetings be pleasurable experiences. If staff meetings are painful experiences, it won't matter how much you threaten people to attend—they won't show up. And why should they? People avoid pain.

Here are our Gathering Guidelines for creating the ultimate staff meeting.

Gathering Guidelines

1. Sit in a circle.

2. There are no "problems"—only "challenges" and "opportunities."

3. There's no such thing as a "complaint"—only "suggestions" with at least two solutions.

4. There are no dumb questions, dumb answers, or dumb ideas.

5. Criticizing, teasing, put-downs, and sarcasm are the only taboos.

6. It's okay to say, "I don't know," or "I changed my mind."

7. If you don't agree, say so and explain your thoughts.

8. It's good to have a mind of your own—use it only when it matters.

9. Keep asking until you really understand.

10. Failure is not fatal.

---

1. Sit in a Circle

I'm not sure why, but it seems that we generate more synergy when a team of people are all sitting in a circle, facing each other, *on the same level*, without a "boss" controlling the meeting. Although an owner, leader, or manager may facilitate the staff meeting, the feeling present is that *we're all in this together; we're all on the same page.*

2. There Are No "Problems"—Only "Challenges" and "Opportunities"

The words we use have an effect and impact on others. If I stand in front of my staff and blurt out, "We have a big *problem* here. This office is a mess, you bunch of pigs," then I'm forcing people to take the defensive: "It's her fault! No, it's his fault!" Instead, if I choose different words, my motive is perceived as different: "Hey, we have a great *opportunity* here. If we can keep this office cleaner, it will create a more productive work environment, we'll be happier, the client will be happier, and we can all make more money." The dirty office becomes a challenge or an opportunity, rather than a problem.

3. There's No Such Thing as a "Complaint"—Only "Suggestions" with at Least Two Solutions

Some people seem to think they were hired to find all the problems in your company or business. They walk around with their imaginary clipboards, making a list of everything that's wrong, and then they share their complaints with anyone and everyone. It's as if they want to dump their complaints onto someone else and say, "If you fixed these problems, I could be brilliant."

Make it part of your company culture that there is no such thing as a complaint. People can make suggestions, but there are two parts of a suggestion. The second part is the solution. Make it a policy that no one can even voice a suggestion unless they've already thought of at least two solutions.

I learned this one from my mother. With eight kids in the family, my mother would often say, "I'm not the complaint department around here. You come back with two solutions, and then we can talk." As little children, we'd pout and stomp off. But what did we go off to do? Find solutions! My mother taught us at an early age, *If it's to be, it's up to me.* Yet there are grown adults who still haven't learned that lesson. They think their job is to find problems and dump them onto others to resolve. Your culture will now teach them to be solution oriented.

David Wagner, author of *Life as a Daymaker*, says that the title on his business card reads "Daymaker" rather than president or CEO. If you ask David what that means, he responds with, "I'm a daymaker—I want to make your day!" David emphasizes that his job is to bring out the best in others, and the best in any situation. David is solution oriented, and this Gathering Guideline will help you and your teammates become that way, too.

4. There Are No Dumb Questions, Dumb Answers, or Dumb Ideas

Nothing diminishes the effectiveness of a staff meeting more than someone rolling their eyes every time another staff member asks a question or makes a comment.

Staff members must let each other know and feel that staff meetings are private, sacred times for connecting with each other and feeling better about themselves and the people they work with. You create that sense of safety by checking your judgments and attitudes at the door and by encouraging each other to share your questions, answers, and ideas freely.

5. Criticizing, Teasing, Put-Downs, and Sarcasm Are the Only Taboos

Staff meetings are not only about communication and relationship building; they're also about brainstorming ideas for continually growing and improving your systems. Brainstorming means letting your creative minds soar, without any boundaries. No idea is too outrageous. That doesn't mean you'll implement the outrageous ideas, but those crazy, over-the-top ideas derived from a creative brainstorming session can certainly spawn other fabulous ideas that could be implemented.

Let's say I happen to work in the same company with my best friend of ten years, and our company is hosting a creative brainstorming session for improving customer service. Let's say that my best friend happens to throw out some wild, crazy idea, which I use as an opportunity to give her a little dig—a little sarcastic joke or comment at her expense. Now, my friend knows I love her and that I'm just showing my usual sarcastic humor. In fact, she may even laugh right along with everyone else. But let me ask you something: Will my friend be as free with her creativity next time? No. Look what I've done to my friend, just so I could get a laugh.

Many of my staff and I have been working together for over twenty years. We often go out to dinner, socialize, and even vacation with each other. At those times, a lot of our dialogue and humor is all about fun put-downs and sarcasm at each other's expense. That's how we have fun with each other, that's our humor, and it's fine when we're out to dinner. But in a staff meeting, it's taboo. And even though we've believed and practiced this in my company for years, I can't tell you how often in a staff meeting I overhear staff members whispering to each other, "Number five, number five!" attempting to remind each other that, *Oh yeah, we're not out to dinner with each other, we're in a staff meeting, and sarcasm is inappropriate.*

6. It's Okay to Say, "I Don't Know" or "I Changed My Mind"

It's important that staff meetings continue to be about communication and team building, not a match of wits and egos. People don't have to be know-it-alls. Sometimes it can be very empowering to hear each other say, "I don't know the answer to that, but why don't we discover the answer or solution together?"

Because it's vital for the growth of your company to be continuously tweaking, changing, and improving your systems, it's also necessary to *change your mind* often. On occasion, a staff member will say to me, "But Winn, you said we could have blue jean Fridays," to which I can then respond with, "I changed my mind." Or, "But Winn, you said I didn't have to attend staff meetings," and I respond with, "I changed my mind."

(I must confess that I love this Gathering Guideline a lot.)

7. If You Don't Agree, Say So and Explain Your Thoughts

Creating a team feeling doesn't mean that everyone has to agree with each other. You're going to disagree, and that's okay.

If you don't agree, then you're encouraged to say so and explain your thoughts. However, in explaining why you don't agree, you can't package your words in the form of a put-down, in sarcasm, or as an attack.

8. It's Good to Have a Mind of Your Own—Use It Only When It Matters

Oh, how staff meetings can sometimes drag on and on. Why? Because people love to hear the sound of their voices. They love to get their two cents in.

Imagine that you're in a staff meeting and another team member is sharing his or her idea about something you don't totally agree with. Eventually, you decide that the idea—although you hadn't considered it before—will probably work just fine. Do you really need to voice your thoughts about the idea? Not always; *only* when it really matters.

9. Keep Asking Until You Really Understand

Golden Rule number four challenges you to *be informed.* Staff meetings are one of the vehicles to help you be informed, and they're the perfect time to ask questions, because you'll be held accountable and expected to know what's going on. If you don't understand something, or need more information, ask questions:

Now, what time is that staff training?

Tell me again, exactly what is the new policy for handling customer complaints?

Keep asking until you really understand.

10. Failure Is Not Fatal

The six words of a failing business are "We've always done it that way." The nature of business is to embrace and cultivate change. However, if you're talking about change, then you're talking about risk. And if you're talking about risk, then you're talking about the possibility of individuals making mistakes, which is why you need to promote the belief that failure is not fatal.

Most companies celebrate successes. Now it's time to start celebrating the mistakes and discoveries that team members make. Why did they make a mistake? Well, maybe it was because they were willing to take a risk, to try something radical, to stretch themselves and thereby grow the company. Create an environment where making a mistake is okay—where failure is not fatal.

I want to share a little side note on this subject, because sometimes people can get confused as to why this Gathering Guideline does not apply to them or their situation. All companies and businesses need to decide which actions and behaviors are fatal, and for which employees could lose their jobs. For example, you may decide that stealing is fatal in your company, whereas gossip may not be.

◼ ◼ ◼

These last two chapters have put a great deal of responsibility back onto every individual working for a company—even those who think they have no power and therefore choose to just whine and complain. You might be thinking that this is quite a bit of information to digest and an awful lot of work to implement. I personally have been at this game for over twenty years in my own business, so let me breathe some hope into your business, career, store, or wherever you go to get a paycheck: What I've shared in chapters 8 and 9 can radically swing the pendulum at work from a negative, toxic environment to a joyful, lovely place where people want to hang out. How?

This book allows nice people to "come out of the closet" and gives them a voice. I envision co-workers and friends sharing and discussing the systems presented in these chapters—systems for building quality relationships by implementing the Golden Rules, systems for improving growth and learning by implementing the Guiding Principles, and systems for communication by implementing the Gathering Guidelines. I picture a nice person sharing this book with a spouse, a friend, or employer, and saying, "See! I'm not weak, I'm NICE!" I picture employees sending the book anonymously to their mean boss with a kind note saying, "We really love working here, and we want to be more productive to make you look good and to make you more money. We believe this book can help you to help us."

My hope is that these last two chapters will help to defuse the all-powerful bosses of the world who are wrecking havoc on poor, dedicated, hardworking employees around the planet. Bottom line, these two chapters prove that by adopting a BE NICE culture, a company will make more money.

I didn't figure this stuff out on my own. My mother and grandmother, along with my many mentors, taught me how to be nice, and they were very specific about it. Perhaps a person you work with didn't have the parenting or mentoring on how to be nice. Perhaps they didn't learn how to get along, how to communicate or negotiate. With the tutoring of this book, and the implementation of the systems shared here, they can begin to learn how to be true adults while at work.

Your Home-Play Assignment:

Self Check, Peer Check, Leader Check

To sustain a culture requires total and complete focus, devotion to the cultural systems, and one more important element: frequent inspecting of the community. Too many times we confuse the words *expect* and *inspect*. What you expect isn't nearly as valuable as what you inspect. Don't assume that people are doing their jobs, don't expect that they're doing their jobs—inspect.

Accountability is huge in a successful organization. We hold ourselves accountable, and we hold each other accountable. We're holding each other accountable to a standard of excellence, and the spirit by which we conduct accountability is one of love, support, and growth. What does that feel like? If you're my peer or my leader, and you're "checking" me, you're looking for the things that I'm doing right, and you're helping me to improve in the areas in which I fall short. You're my coach.

For your home-play assignment, make a poster of this if you need to remind yourself and your team:

Praise in public.

Reprimand in private.

Let's Start a BE NICE Revolution

"When the heart is set right, then the personal life is cultivated;
when the personal life is cultivated, then the family life is regulated;
when the family life is regulated, then the national life is orderly;
and when the national life is orderly, then there is peace in this world."
—Confucius

While witnessing life's tragedies, heartbreaks, discrimina-
tions, and injustices, how often do you catch yourself saying, "Someone should do something about that problem . . .
but not me. I couldn't possibly make a difference"?

To see yourself as small and powerless serves no one. This entire
book has been about tiny shifts in thought, perception, belief, and
action. It's been about helping you realize that *you* are the person who
can and should do something about the injustices of the world. The
"something" you can do is what this chapter is all about: starting a BE
NICE revolution.

It takes just one person to start a BE NICE campaign. *You* can decide
that you will no longer participate in a lifestyle of being mean to people, in big ways, small ways, overtly, covertly, intentionally, or uninten-
tionally. *You* can decide that you will no longer let good service and
kind words go unnoticed. *You* can decide to show your appreciation for
every act of kindness, no matter how small or large. There are as many
ways to start a BE NICE revolution as there are individual people on
this planet, because every one of us can decide to make a difference in
our own way.

You Don't Have to Tell Me

How many times have you heard someone preface their dialogue or action by making the announcement, "You know I'm a (Christian, Buddhist, or any other term that's meant to indicate religiosity or niceness)"? When I hear someone say that, I want to respond with, "If you really are a (Christian, Buddhist, etc.), you won't need to tell me. Your words and actions should make the point."

That same scenario applies to your BE NICE revolution. Rather than running around telling everyone that you're a nice person, or that you've launched a BE NICE revolution, why not let your words and actions broadcast your new intentions? Let people see that you've become more sensitive to the role you play and more aware of the influence you have on others. Let people experience the conviction and change in you. As Gandhi said, "We must become the change we wish to see in the world."

Choose Your Own Path

I have a confession to make. For months, my good friend George had been pleading with me to go see a scary movie with him and our other good friend, Kate. He thought it would be fun. I can honestly say that it had been ten years or more since I'd seen a movie like that, but—although I can't believe I actually went along with it—against my better judgment, I did.

I'll avoid a lengthy explanation about how it affected me, but let's just say that the movie accomplished what it was meant to do: it disturbed me. As hard as I tried to walk out of that movie theater, shrug it off, turn to my friends, and playfully say, "Hey, wanna get something to eat?" I couldn't. I was altered. In fact, I turned to Kate and yelled at her, "Why would you do that to me?" She just stared at me as if I'd turned into a total stranger. It took me a good hour before I felt a little like myself again (at which point I picked up the phone and called her to apologize). It was probably another couple of days before I could make sense of what had happened to me. Here's what I came up with.

Different things have different effects on people. For example, I can't eat nuts because my body will have an allergic reaction, but other people can eat nuts all day long. I can't see scary movies because my body, mind, and soul will have a negative reaction, but George has no problems with scary movies. In fact, he compares seeing them to riding a roller coaster.

Here's my point. Each of us must choose the path that works for us. What works for me is different than what works for you. I can't eat nuts, but maybe you can, so it makes no sense for me to tell you that you can't.

Your path and your BE NICE revolution are yours—let other people discover theirs. However, if you're looking for some ideas to get you started, here are a few of my favorites.

Host Your Own Awards Show

It's amazing the number of award shows that pop up every year. We have award shows for acting, for fashion, for hairstyling, and for musical talent. We have award shows for people who were born with good physical genes—as if they had some choice in the matter. Our society even rewards workaholics. Parents could spend all of their time at work, ignoring their family, abandoning their parental duties to make money, and society will pat them on the back: "What good providers they are."

How about if you started hosting your own awards show on a daily basis? How? Start recognizing and rewarding people who are nice. Look for, thank, acknowledge, and take care of them. Remember, that which you focus on starts to grow.

Choose Nice Companies

When it comes to spending money, you have plenty of options. Some people love to purchase and wear designer labels and quality goods, while others love to search for great bargains at a thrift store. Some people like to splurge for front-row tickets to a Broadway play, and others enjoy seeing the hottest movies at their neighborhood theater. Yes, you can make decisions with your head about how and where to spend your money, but you can also start making decisions with your gut. How do you feel about that company? What's behind their product or service? In your desire to start a BE NICE revolution, you can choose to spend your money in ways that support companies, organizations, and individuals who believe in the importance of being nice.

I like to know something about a company's culture and who owns it. Are they good to their employees? Do they provide a fair, safe, harmonious work environment? Is their product environmentally friendly? Are they honest and filled with integrity? Do they give back to their communities?

To tell you the truth, I hope that people research my company that way. I want them to know the inner workings of who we are and what we stand for, and that we do more than just provide a product or service. I want them to get inside and ask my people if I'm a nice guy, if they love their job, if they adore their co-workers. We work hard to create and practice what I've shared in this book, so I want people to investigate and tell us how we're doing.

In addition to being proactive in asking about a company's behind-the-scenes activities, an easy way to research a company, its products, and its philosophy is through the Internet. Visit a company's Web site and read its mission statements and philosophies. Every company is designed to make a profit, so look beyond that. Do they mention how they treat their people, or how they provide support for those less fortunate? Are they environmentally aware? What about their hiring practices—are they truly nondiscriminatory? Are all of these areas reflected in their mission statement and overall vision?

I look for nice companies to use as mentors and role models for my own company, and so that I can "reward" them by choosing to spend money there. I checked out a couple of companies online because I heard, either through friends who worked there or through press about them, that they were nice companies. My motive in mentioning these companies is not as an endorsement of their product or service, because frankly that's not my role. I merely want to point out that there are companies doing nice things for their employees, their customers, or their communities, and we can all learn from them, find companies who do similar things, and choose to spend our money with them in support of the nice things they do.

I'm sure that if I were to name specific companies, there'd be one or one thousand people who'd want to dispute my perceived endorsement. Since I don't want the message to be lost by challenging people to weigh in as to whether or not they believe a company to be nice, I'll simply describe the attributes that I admire most.

I researched one company that not only pledges 1 percent of its annual sales to environmental protection and restoration, but it also offers its employees five days of paid annual leave to volunteer at their children's schools. In addition, employees can maintain their benefits and salary for up to two months while they work for a nonprofit organization.

I was very impressed with another company whose Web site describes its commitment to doing good business while being part of the global and local community. That company also offers paid leave to employees who work with nonprofits and provides service to schools, community centers, parks, and youth programs.

I know of several companies that provide daycare centers, not for their customers but for their staff, so parents don't have to be far from their children. For the single parent who can't afford daycare, and can't afford to work half days, this is a huge benefit that perceivably has nothing to do with creating a better product for the company.

As you begin looking further into the companies whose products and services you currently use, or those you don't use, I'm sure you'll discover, as I did, that doing this kind of research is quite educational and fun. I found it fascinating to know that the company who makes some of the clothes I purchase is actually very active in its community and that its philosophies are similar to my own. In a very real sense, my discovery of this company's responsible approach to doing business made me feel good about myself for purchasing its product.

Choose Nice Nonprofits

In addition to researching nice for-profit companies so that you can support them by spending money with them, I also want to challenge you to look for and support nice nonprofit organizations. There are amazing organizations that do amazing things, and they'd all love to have your attention and participation. When choosing where to donate your time and money, how about embracing a couple of organizations whose sole mission is to cultivate a BE NICE society? Here are some great examples.

The Pay It Forward Foundation was established to educate and inspire young students to realize that they can change the world and to provide them with opportunities to do so. By bringing author Catherine Ryan Hyde's vision and related materials into classrooms internationally, students and their teachers are encouraged to formulate their own ideas of how they can "pay it forward." Students have the opportunity to identify what they consider to be the challenges of their communities. They tackle such problems as homelessness, pollution, youth violence, literacy issues, the loneliness experienced by long-term hospital and nursing home patients, and the alienation of today's at-risk youth from the community. You can visit their Web site at www.PayItForwardFoundation.org.

The Random Acts of Kindness Foundation inspires people to practice kindness and pass it on to others. Through the dissemination of ideas and the development of materials and programs, they've helped "kindness coordinators"—educators, students, community members, faith groups, service clubs, and others—to incorporate kindness into thousands of schools and communities. The foundation believes that as people tap into their own generous human spirit and share kindness with one another, they discover for themselves the power of kindness to effect positive change. When kindness is expressed, healthy relationships are created, community connections are nourished, and people are inspired to pass it on. You can check them out at www.ActsOfKindness.org.

The Daymaker Movement was launched by my good friend David Wagner, whom I've mentioned in this book several times. Its Web site says that there's nothing to join, just an attitude to adopt. The Daymaker Movement asks the question, "What if you could change the world by making someone's day?" It suggests that you just notice the people you encounter each day and provide a small gesture to make their day. When you give others the quality of attention that makes them feel important, smart, beautiful, or unique, it's nearly impossible to focus on your own problems. Being a daymaker can have profound effects, offering you a way to significantly impact your community and generating a ripple effect that can change the world. Being a daymaker creates a tipping point in which the pendulum is biased in the direction of kindness, care, love, and joy. You can find out more by visiting www.DaymakerMovement.com.

Volunteer Match is a nonprofit organization that can help you get yourself active and involved. This online service helps volunteers connect with community service organizations across the United States, offering over thirty thousand ways to serve. Check it out and chart your path for service at www.VolunteerMatch.com.

Reward Nice People

It's amazing that some people will have a bad experience with a rude waiter and instantly complain or write a letter. For the tiniest infraction of rudeness or meanness, they'll loudly announce their displeasure. Yet all of us experience niceness and meet nice people every single day, and do nothing to reward it when it happens. We say nothing to someone who smiles at us. We write no letters to hotel managers when we experience a pleasant front-desk employee. We don't compliment an airline flight attendant as we leave the plane and say, "You were so nice. Thanks!"

When a person is mean, for some reason we give them priority. We hurry to accommodate their needs. Does being mean get the job or task done quicker? Yes, many times it does—which is why people use that strategy. To me, it's the same strategy that some parents use when they verbally or physically abuse their children to get them to do what they want. Why do parents do it? Because it works. It can be very effective. But it's not nice, it's certainly not good parenting, and I doubt that it creates nicer children.

Let's turn that around. The next time you experience a really nice waitress who goes out of her way to brighten up your day, reward her. Maybe you could choose to leave an outrageous tip, and as you're leaving the restaurant, say something like, "You were really nice. Thanks!" so she connects the big tip to being nice.

You could start a letter-writing campaign to support people who are nice. In fact, I'd like to propose that for every "You did me wrong" letter you write, you must also write at least ten "You were amazing and nice" letters.

Here are a few examples of letters you could write to compliment someone's niceness. They're short, sweet, and took only a few minutes to compose.

Dear Restaurant Owner,

Last night my family and I had dinner at your restaurant, and Ijust had to tell you how impressed we were with our waiter, JohnSmith. He was friendly, polite, and seemed to anticipate our every need. His excellent service added so much to our dining experience. He was one of the nicest waiters we've ever met, and he helped make it one of the nicest evenings we've spent in a long time. We look forward to coming back again soon!

Dear Hotel Manager,

I recently spent a few nights at your hotel, and it was one of the most delightful experiences I've ever had. Your staff members were so nice! Everyone I met, from the lovely young woman who checked me in upon arrival, to the doorman who hailed my cab when I left, went way beyond "just doing their job." They were friendly, outgoing, and always cheerful. They smiled and spoke to me whenever I passed by. When I asked for directions to various parts of the hotel, they didn't just tell me, they showed me to my destination. I can't remember ever feeling so welcomed at a hotel before.

Dear Corporation Owner,

I recently had the opportunity to do business with your company, and the experience was amazing. Your facilities were immaculate, the products I needed were easy to locate, and everyone I came in contact with was courteous, helpful, and eager to please. I haven't stopped telling my friends about the quality of your organization, and I look forward to doing business with you in the future.

A friend of mine told me that while in a consumer awareness class in college, he received an interesting assignment. His professor asked the class to write five complaint letters, and then she taught them how to make the letters more "effective." My friend suffered through the lecture until the end, then raised his hand and asked when they'd be taught how to write five "compliment" letters. The professor was outraged until others in the class spoke up, and she finally agreed to the option. It's my friend's understanding that this professor presents both types of letters in her classes today.

Boycott Shows and Films That Aren't Nice

A BE NICE revolution must be more about acknowledging, celebrating, and accentuating all the niceness you find than about pointing your finger at the not-nice. Having said that, it certainly couldn't hurt the morale of us nice guys if we put a little bit of energy into standing up to the not-nice. I know I wouldn't be opposed to taking one for the team by boycotting those who are bent on spreading their misery and gloom.

What if we all boycotted television shows that give people a platform to put other people down, for the entire world to see? These type of shows pop up more and more, it seems, and they give mean people a voice. Or at least they give decent people an opportunity to be mean, and unfortunately they go for it. Hey, we all do mean things on occasion, but not in front of a television camera.

I know I've mentioned negative talk shows in this book several times, and there are several of them with hosts who all choose to make a living by bringing out the worst in people. I don't personally know any of them, but in my mind I have a very clear picture of these talk show hosts driving home each night in their expensive cars, to their expensive homes, after having left a family in shambles in their studios, while millions of television viewers took that into their private living rooms. I can honestly say that these hosts have never made a dime off of me, but I do know people who help pay their high-priced salaries because they choose to watch those shows.

Avoid turning on the television and being content to watch whatever appears. Take a stand. Be clear about your BE NICE purpose and intentions, and make sure that the choices you make are in line with your intentions. Make sure your behavior matches what you value. Choose to watch television shows that inspire you, lighten your mood, educate you, make you laugh, and do all that without degrading others or giving mean, nasty people a platform.

When it comes to which shows and films to watch and which to avoid, it's true that you're just one television viewer and movie ticket purchaser. Your choice to not watch certain shows may or may not make a difference in television ratings, but it will most assuredly make a monumental difference in your ratings as a nice person.

Support Nice Celebrities

People become famous for all sorts of reasons, and their fame can last for fifteen minutes or a lifetime. In the matter of our BE NICE revolution, I'm most interested in what an individual does with his or her celebrity. I tend to be more attracted to movie stars' talent when I hear that they're also nice people or that they do amazing things with their star power.

Let's face it, a movie star can make good things happen just by picking up the phone. You and I might have to work a little more to have the same impact. Since I know firsthand how difficult it can be sometimes to make a difference, I'm always thrilled to hear of celebrities who've chosen to use their star power in worthwhile ways. If they make that choice, then I can make the choice to support them—I'll pay money to see their movies (not the violent ones), I'll watch their television shows, I'll buy their music, and I'll see them in concert.

Although there are thousands of celebrities who do good things with their name and power, those who come to mind include the following:

Paul Newman, sole owner of Newman's Own, donates all of his after-tax profits and royalties for educational and charitable purposes. Since 1982, he's given more than $150 million to thousands of charities. You'd better believe that I buy his salad dressings, popcorn, and pasta sauce. As long as he churns out recipes, I'll continue to buy his products. (For more information, check out www.NewmansOwn.com.)

Leeza Gibbons has created Leeza's Place, an intimate and safe setting where those newly diagnosed with any kind of memory disorder and their caregivers can get education, empowerment, and energy to help them with their difficult journey. When her mother was diagnosed with Alzheimer's disease, Leeza promised to use her story to educate and inspire others. Leeza is known as the nicest woman in Hollywood, and now I can be a nice guy by being one of her cheerleaders and supporters. (For more information, visit www.LeezasPlace.org.)

Both **Elizabeth Taylor** and **Elton John**—as well as many other famous and influential people—have used their names and celebrity to create AIDS organizations. I've always loved Miss Taylor's films, and I purchase anything that Elton John produces. I adore both of them for taking on such an issue, and I'll continue to be their number one fan. (Check out www.ElizabethTaylorAIDSFoundation.org and www.ejaf.org.)

Roughly forty thousand babies are born with cardiovascular defects each year. Thanks to **Larry King** and his lovely wife **Shawn**, who contributed their name and prestige to create the Larry King Cardiac Foundation, many people will be properly educated, and many others will benefit. Although I'm always fascinated with the guests who appear on *Larry King Live*, I'm even more fascinated knowing what Larry and Shawn do with their celebrity. (Find out more at www.lkcf.org.)

I don't know about you, but I was in love with **Audrey Hepburn** from the moment I first saw her in *Roman Holiday*. When I later learned of her work on behalf of ill-treated and suffering children around the world, I was even more in love. In Audrey's words, "I speak for those children who cannot speak for themselves, children who have absolutely nothing but their courage and their smiles, their wits and their dreams." That just warms my heart like you cannot believe. Although Audrey Hepburn is no longer with us, her work continues in numerous ways, through the efforts of the Audrey Hepburn Children's Fund. (Check it out at www.AudreyHepburn.com.)

I could go on and on, but my humble advice is that you use an Internet search site to type in the name of your own favorite celebrities and learn how they choose to use their power. Then you can use *your* power by deciding whether or not they're still your favorite celebrity, or even more so.

Acknowledge Nice Co-Workers: "Caught Ya!"

Another way to spread this BE NICE movement is to take it to your workplace and acknowledge people in your company or organization who are nice. Reward it. If you're in control of people's advancement at work, you can even base raises and promotions not just on a person's productivity, but also on whether or not that person is nice.

Why should you promote and celebrate workers who are nice? First of all, I believe it's their job to be nice, and you want to celebrate people who are doing their jobs. Second, a nice person's participation in your organization can improve *everything*, including customer service, customer loyalty, staff morale, teamwork—you name it. To spread our BE NICE revolution, let's bring "being nice" out of the workplace closet.

Here's one of my favorite ways to recognize niceness and bring more fun into a workplace. In every single location of my company, and in many other businesses I know of, we have what we call our "Caught Ya!" board. Near the Caught Ya! board, we keep preprinted three-by-five-inch cards with the caption, "Caught Ya!" on the top. Whenever a staff member sees another staff member doing something wonderful for a customer or co-worker, they're encouraged to "write them up." A Caught Ya! message could read something like, "To Janet: Your smiling face and jokes are what I most look forward to when I walk into work each day." Or, "To Derrick: Thanks for surprising me by cleaning up the stock room."

It's so easy to catch someone doing something wrong. Someone in your organization makes a mistake, and you say, "Aha! I caught ya!" Remember, you'll promote, encourage, and create what you look for and focus on. If you look for people to make mistakes, they will. If you think it's your job to be a policing agent and catch people doing things wrong, then that's what you'll encourage people to do, and they won't let you down. How about trying a different approach? How about encouraging your entire organization to catch each other doing things *right?*

My recommendation is that you display the Caught Ya! board in a common area where staff members always hang out, such as the lunch area or break room. Those areas often turn into "Gossip Central," because that's where those people I like to call "spoons" hang out— they're back there stirring things up. A Caught Ya! board in that area can dispel the negative chitchat that often festers there.

A while back, while visiting a company for which I was consulting, I discovered their Caught Ya! board in their staff lunch area. I thoroughly enjoyed watching person after person make their way over to that board and stand there for many minutes, reading about all the wonderful things their colleagues were doing. In fact, one girl told me that the day before, she had seen another team member fall behind in her work, so without being asked, she jumped in to help her catch up. She said that when she arrived the next morning (the day I was there), she looked at the Caught Ya! board and saw that the other girl had written her up and posted how fabulous she thought this girl was for helping. Once she read the kind words written about her, what was she then motivated to do that day? You got it—to help as many people as she could.

If you like this idea, how about creating a family Caught Ya! board at home? Families can be so busy, and they rarely get the time together they long for. Plus, Mom and Dad can easily fall into the trap of recognizing and punishing all the bad things their children do. Imagine how a family's dynamics could change if Mom and Dad came home from a hectic day, glanced at the family Caught Ya! board, and read, "Hey Matt: Thanks for sticking up for me in front of those kids at school today. You're the best brother a girl could ever have!"

Give Back to Your Community

One of the most important and meaningful ways to spread your BE NICE revolution is to embrace people who are less fortunate. Why? Because it's a nice thing to do, it's the right thing to do, and it sets up a wonderful opportunity to bring out the niceness in everyone involved.

Over the past twenty years, my company and its wonderful staff have chosen to get involved in all sorts of different causes and charities, including AIDS, breast cancer research, mental health, homelessness, firefighters, battered women, abused children, the elderly, the 9/11 tragedy, leukemia, and more. Were these all causes and charities that I chose? Well, some of them were causes that I personally am passionate about, so I rallied up my team to help me make a difference. But the majority of our philanthropic pursuits were the causes and charities that individual staff members were passionate about.

When you ask your family, friends, staff and fellow workers what they care about, and then you join their cause and help them make a difference, you'll cultivate better relationships and sustain a healthy work culture like you've never seen before. And how do you find out what causes are important to your family, friends, staff, and your co-workers? You ask them.

At my school in Provo, Utah, for over ten years a sweet elderly woman by the name of Gladys came to us on the same day, every single week for her shampoo set. Gladys was in her eighties, about five feet tall, and absolutely adorable.

One day, I was in the reception area of my school, and sweet, old Gladys came up to me with four dollars in her hand, which was the price of our shampoo set. She held the four dollars up and asked me, "Winn, how much hair color can I get for four dollars?" Amused, I stepped back and replied, "Gladys, after ten years you now want to color your hair? Have you got a special occasion coming up?" Gladys softly gazed at me and said, "It's my husband's funeral tomorrow."

With that, I unthinkingly blurted out, "Gladys, your hair color is free. From now on, all of your services are free. In fact, NO SENIOR CITIZEN WILL EVER PAY MONEY IN THIS SCHOOL AGAIN!" It was one of those stupid business decisions that one makes based on pure emotion. Soon, it seemed that the small clientele of perhaps thirty senior citizens went home and e-mailed all their friends: "FREE services at Winn's school!" All of a sudden, hundreds of senior citizens began coming in for services, all for free.

I started to receive cards, cookies, quilts, and marriage proposals for the great-granddaughters. Was it a smart business decision? No, it was stupid. But it was the right thing to do. Have you ever noticed that sometimes life comes to you and asks, "Will you do it? Are you willing?" And you respond with, "This is *not* what I had planned. This is *not* part of my business plan . . . but, yes, I'll do it." Why? Simply because it's the right thing to do. And how did this very simple story affect our team and our company? It sent out a message that we can and do make a difference in our bigger community. We take care of each other, we take care of our customers, we're here to serve, and we're nice.

□ □ □

Whenever I ask an audience, "How many of you believe that knowledge equals power?" almost every hand goes up. Yes, knowledge can equal power, but only if it's coupled with ACTION.

People sit through a training session or seminar, frantically scribbling pages of notes, but I often wonder what happens to those notes after the seminar ends. Do people implement the information? Do they do things differently? Are they somehow changed for the better? As I've shared previously, the purpose of education is to change behavior. If nothing changes, then all the education and knowledge you attain equals nothing. To know something and not implement it is the same thing as not knowing it.

As you go out into the world with your BE NICE revolution, please remember this simple formula:

$$Knowledge + Action = Power$$

I've often been accused of *Ready, FIRE, aim,* rather than *Ready, AIM, fire.* On the other hand, I know people who *Ready, aim, aim, aim, aim, aim* . . . and they never fire. They never make a move. Before you put this book down, I challenge you to take action now, make a move, and do something toward starting your BE NICE revolution. Now that you've acquired the knowledge, *do something* with it. That's your final home-play assignment.

Your Home-Play Assignment:
Do Something!

Make a move, even if you're not sure it's the right move. You'll figure it out, and by making tiny shifts in your thoughts and actions, you'll soon be building your own confidence and self-esteem, growing your circle of nice, healing your relationships, and making a difference everywhere you go. By making the simplest of moves, you'll be on your way to becoming a BE NICE master.

Sometimes it's difficult to raise money and awareness in order to make a difference, but your nice actions alone toward family, friends, acquaintances, and total strangers will promote the simplicity of making a difference in other ways. If you trust that you have a kind heart, then believe that the actions you take will make a difference.

While you're being nice to others, don't forget to discover and celebrate the niceties that other people offer. Never underestimate the impact of your acknowledgment of a person's niceness. It could be the only acknowledgment they ever receive. That's huge.

Remember, together we can make the world a nicer place. When that happens, no one—not even the nice guys—will "finish last." In a BE NICE world, everybody wins.

P.S. — My goal is to be known, more than anything else, as a nice guy. So I have one last assignment for you. If you would, please check back with me, and if I've gotten off track, kindly remind me to BE NICE.

ACKNOWLEDGMENTS

I am such a product of my mentors and have studied and applied their teachings so much that my thoughts in this book will border between plagiarism and personal experience. But to my many mentors I just want to say,

I did what you intended for me to do.
I took your teachings and I ran with them.

I did not keep to myself that which I learned from you. I implemented your beautiful wisdom into every area of my life. I hope you will recognize your teachings, not just in this book but also in my career, in my relationships, in my company's policies and procedures manual, in my conversations with total strangers, and in my community.

Louise Hay — When I began my journey of "this works and that doesn't," I needed my mentors to be women. Perhaps because of some past experiences, I wasn't very open to what a male mentor would have to say. Louise immediately became top billing in my world, and I wanted to share her message with anyone and everyone. Her books became required reading for my staff, and her seminars and audio programs became regular events in my life for years. As a speaker and seminar leader, I learned just as much from Louise about how to handle an audience as I did from the information she presented. I remember very clearly a woman during one question-and-answer time who recounted through her tears how everyone in her life thought she was worthless. Her husband thought she was worthless because she was fat. Her children thought she was worthless because she was lazy. Her boss thought she was worthless because of some other reason. Finally, after sighing from boredom, Louise interrupted the woman's "They all believe I'm worthless" story by saying, "Well, maybe they're all right." The entire audience gasped, as if to say, "Louise! Why would you say that to this poor woman? How insensitive!" The woman stopped her dribble and said, "What?" Louise continued, "Maybe they're all correct. Maybe you are worthless." After going back and forth with this exercise, it became very apparent to the audience, and eventually apparent to the woman, what Louise was trying to say. This master of educators didn't buy the woman's tale of worthlessness, and that opened the door for the woman to consider an alternative self-belief. Many times since then I have thought to myself that although I may not have the highest regard for myself, that doesn't mean other people agree with me. Sometimes we have to trust and believe it when other people see us as valuable, even if we don't see it ourselves. Thanks, Louise.

Og Mandino – Listening to Og Mandino either live or on audio was like listening to Grandpa tell stories. I always felt safe with his words and his voice. Many years ago, I was fortunate to attend a seminar given by Og Mandino in San Diego. Someone asked, "If you had only one piece of advice on how to be happy, what would it be?" Og effortlessly answered, "Just imagine that every person you come into contact with is wearing a label that says, MAKE ME FEEL IMPORTANT." I think about that *a lot*, and I've related that story hundreds of times.

Oprah Winfrey – Like everyone in her television audience, I watched Oprah transform herself, her show, and eventually millions of people. I have no inside knowledge of what went on behind the scenes, but it seemed as though perhaps Oprah was making monumental discoveries about herself and was growing by leaps and bounds. Along with her own growth, she facilitated the growth of millions of people who watched her show. I suspect she took a profound risk in going from the genre of a negative, gossipy talk show to something that actually benefited and uplifted her audience. In my distant perception of Oprah, I saw someone who had the courage to divorce herself from sensationalized negativity and instead teach an entire country about personal integrity, honest relationships, and community accountability. I figure we all have an audience for whom we must take responsibility, and I thank Oprah for the example.

Marianne Williamson – Where do I start? When I say I attended hundreds of Marianne's seminars, I'm not exaggerating. To say that I own a hundred Marianne Williamson lectures on audiotape would also not be an exaggeration. I volunteered at any charitable event that Marianne could come up with. I answered the phone, licked envelopes, washed dishes, and even had my own canister donation route. My favorite Christmas present to give (and a favorite for the person to receive) is a case filled with twenty Marianne Williamson tapes. Why am I such a student of Marianne's? It took me years to understand the devotion, but I eventually realized that what she had to share was exactly what I was looking for, without realizing I was looking for anything. When it comes to a belief in a higher power, a belief in myself exactly as I am, and a belief in the goodness of people, Marianne provides a foundation for all of that, and she does it with humor, confidence, and loudness. Yeah, God has a sense of humor, he doesn't mind that I too am loud, and I thank Marianne for teaching me that.

John Bradshaw — Yes, I needed a spiritual curriculum, but I also needed a clinical one. Why not cover all the bases, I thought. I studied and memorized John's book *The Family*, which armed me with some facts and logical arguments about human nature. I learned that I was not a freak of nature—just as many people believe they are. Instead, I'm a product of nature and of the society in which I live. Understanding that didn't make me succumb to my lowly state of self-worth; rather, it helped me understand how I got there and what I could do to change it. Along with a thousand other people, I attended a seminar with John Bradshaw, and the entire convention hall was set up in circles of six chairs, each with a box of tissue in the middle. That discovery stopped me dead in my tracks and almost made me want to escape the conference, but I trusted John because of his books and his PBS specials. I can't tell you how much I resisted needing those tissues, and I almost made it to the very end of the day. But then John asked us to have our child self write a letter to our adult self to share and explain our child needs—only he asked us to write the letter with a crayon, and to use our opposite hand. An hour later, I had before me what looked like the scribbling of a very young, little boy, only it was my writings expressing my needs; needs that only I could provide. I pounced onto that box of tissue and have had a very fond spot in my heart for John ever since.

Gerald Jampolski — Children have always been major mentors for me. I'm forty-four years old and the best compliment a person can give to me is, "You're such a little kid!" At family parties, I always want to sit at the kids' table, be their center of attention, play their games, and be the favorite uncle. Gerald's book, *Teach Only Love*, outlines the lessons taught by children who are dealing with very adult experiences: disease and dying. Gerald acknowledges and celebrates that children are his mentors as well, and I was so grateful to come along for the ride.

George Melton and Will Garcia – These two men had the courage to take on a disease that most people didn't even want to admit existed: AIDS. In the early 1980s, both were afflicted with this terrible nightmare and they somehow figured out that they didn't have to lie down and die, as popular opinion dictated. Instead, they chose to take a spiritual journey, which proved to diminish the power of AIDS in their bodies, as well as the power of AIDS in the media. They sold their belongings, bought a motor home, and began traveling the country to selflessly share what they'd discovered. They brought hope when hope wasn't even a consideration. After hearing them speak, I approached them for more words, more proof, more hope, because I was losing close friends. They gave me a piece of paper—their list of suggested reading material. At the top of that list was *You Can Heal Your Life* by Louise Hay. I bought that book the very next day, along with many other books on their list, and then carried that list around with me for seventeen years. In fact, I had that piece of paper with me the day I met Louise Hay. I have since taken that old, yellowed, tattered, precious document and had it framed.

Leo Buscaglia – What a lovely, gentle man who seemed to laugh while he spoke. No matter what Leo had to say or write about, I was always interested, simply because he seemed to believe it so strongly. His audio recording about his family's day at the beach, in honor of his father, brought me tears of joy and made me understand the profound love that my own father has, and has always had, for my mother, my siblings, and me. That's huge.

SPECIAL ACKNOWLEDGMENTS

As I wrapped up the four-year process of writing this book, several people told me, "You should feel so proud of yourself for accomplishing such a task." Indeed, I feel very proud of the personal proclamation that this book represents. However, I am continually mindful that any person's creativity is a collaboration of many, many people. Therefore, all of the following individuals should also feel proud.

To my romantic friends (some of whom I'm also related to), Dennis James, Dianne Ingram, Brennan Claybaugh, Denny and Chris Claybaugh, Kate Caussey, Sandy and Rosie Matos, Michael and Nina Galvin, Tova Stroman, George Morales, Bo Powell, Brett Jarvis, and Giulio Veglio, who all told me I'd have a powerful book long before one word was written.

To Johnny Flanagan and Michael Broadhead, who reentered my life at a time when I needed caring friends from my past to assist me through writing this book. You made me feel that the craziness and insecurity of my past had only served to make me into a confident adult, and you helped me to believe that I had something to share.

To my coaches Vivienne Mackinder, Tommy Callahan, Sam Brocato, Marianne Dougherty, and Sasha Rash, who read manuscripts that weren't ready for everyone's eyes, yet treated my writings with tenderness and respect.

To my heroes Leeza Gibbons, Larry and Shawn King, John Paul and Eloise DeJoria, David Wagner, and Catherine Ryan Hyde, whose mere interest in this book provided hours and hours of passion for writing, as well as the motivation to finish.

To my cheerleaders Donna and Bill Waite, Laini Reeves, Melissa Yamaguchi, Joan Harrison, Jill Kohler, James Morrison, Shari Polk, Michael Toth, Dean Banowetz, Susan Papageorgio, Stella Davis, Jayne Cloo, Kazhal Showani, Tami LeCleur, Shawn Trujillo, Angie Katsanevas, Eric Jansson, Luke Jacobellis, Michael Turnage, Sue Keith, Vance Moody, John DiJulius, Ray Civello, Debra Dietrich, Sharon Gault, Jimy Angel, and Lisa Quateman, who offered frankness and reinforcing words of, "Well, of course you're writing a book!" Sometimes, all it takes is friendship to inspire someone's creativity.

To my extensive "families" at Von Curtis and Paul Mitchell, who have earnestly tried to live a BE NICE lifestyle for years. You have all provided me with love and support (and lots of funny anecdotes), and together we've experimented with the principles shared in this book. Also, to my day-to-day comrades, Jennifer Johnson and Josh Corso, who enthusiastically printed and distributed the last fifty versions of my scribblings. I never underestimate the valuable role you have played in my personal and professional happiness.

To Christian Gurgone and Genie O'Malley at Authors of Unity, Ramey Warren Black at Media Savvy, and to all those who chose to say "yes" to this project, even though I was Joe Schmo off the street.

To Gail Fink; while some might treat you as "just an editor," to me—through the process of writing this book—you've been a tutor, a collaborator, and a friend.

And finally, I thank my siblings; my nieces and nephews; and especially my very humble, loving, and wise parents, Donn and Jeanne Claybaugh.

ABOUT THE AUTHOR

Winn **Claybaugh** has been the owner of hair salons and beauty academies since 1983. He is the founder and co-owner (along with John Paul DeJoria) of **Paul Mitchell The School**, with several locations throughout the United States. Winn is widely recognized as a leader in his industry; in 2004, the North American Hairstyling Awards (NAHA) named him to their Hall of Leaders for his outstanding contributions to the hair and beauty industry.

Since 1989, Winn has traveled extensively around the country, working as an educator and consultant for several industries. He has been the National Motivational Expert for **Paul Mitchell,** the hair product company. He has worked with thousands of private businesses and their staffs, including companies such as **Vidal Sassoon, the Irvine Company, Entertainment Tonight, Mattel,** *For Rent* **magazine, Structure/Limited Express,** and many other businesses from hospitals to apartment communities.

In its November 1997 "Super Heroes" section, *American Salon* magazine called Winn a "mover of mountains" and "Mr. Fix-it." It has been said of Winn's programs that, rather than just getting people excited, he offers a solid plan to increase productivity and attitude. His **Shot-In-The-Arm** event and **Developing Leadership Pizzazz** seminar have been attended by top executives, clinical psychologists, salespeople of every sort, day care providers, housewives, and people from every walk of life who are looking for a new approach to personal motivation. Winn's humor and rapport with audiences create enthusiasm and momentum to help businesses get motivated and focused for greater success. His seminars are designed to empower leaders to create teamwork among their people and motivation for themselves.

Winn has also served as vice president of the AIDS Relief Fund for Beauty Professionals and has been involved in other fundraising projects for City of Hope. He resides in Laguna Beach, California.

Gail Fink is a freelance writer and editor with more than thirty years of professional experience. Her writing and editing credits include all types of media, from books and audiotapes to newspaper and magazine columns, Web sites, e-newsletters, and online continuing education courses. She covers a wide variety of topics, including personal development, spirituality, business, health, nutrition, travel, medicine, and more. She resides in San Diego, California, with her husband Robert.

▪ ▪ ▪

RESOURCES

If you're committed to being nice, you'll want to take advantage of these powerful resources from Winn Claybaugh...

Connecting to My Future!

A Learning and Planning Guide for Future and New Salon Professionals

By Winn Claybaugh

Connecting to My Future is a success guide that will help you get focused and stay focused on the steps to creating the career of your dreams in the beauty industry. Whether you've just started school or are a working professional, *Connecting to My Future* is your map to successfully "playing" within the beauty business.

Packed with proven strategies and essential tips, *Connecting to My Future* will help you shift your thinking, sharpen your skills, connect with your potential, and take control of your success.

To order your copy, please contact:

Order by phone:	(866) 302-5576 toll free
Order online:	www.PaulMitchellTheSchool.com
Order by mail:	PAUL MITCHELL THE SCHOOL
	The Store
	1226 West South Jordan Pkwy, Unit C200
	South Jordan, UT 84095
E-mail:	info@PaulMitchellTheSchool.com

Connecting to My Future..$19.95

Connecting to My Future!

Book on CD

Take your learning to the next level with this entertaining 8-CD series, which includes the entire book on audio. *Connecting to My Future* **Book on CD** features energetic introductions from celebrity professionals like Robert Cromeans and John Paul DeJoria. Learn from master talent from around the industry in candid interviews led by Winn Claybaugh. *Connecting to My Future* **Book on CD** is a perfect learning tool to add to your library.

To order, please contact:

Order by phone:	(866) 302-5576 toll free
Order online:	www.PaulMitchellTheSchool.com
Order by mail:	PAUL MITCHELL THE SCHOOL
	The Store
	1226 West South Jordan Pkwy, Unit C200
	South Jordan, UT 84095
E-mail:	info@PaulMitchellTheSchool.com

Connecting to My Future **Book on CD** $99.95

MASTERS

Audio Club

MASTERS is a monthly audio program featuring interviews, success secrets, and business-building presentations by the absolute best leaders in the salon and beauty industry.

Your subscription includes one CD per month featuring different masters, heroes, icons, legends, and mentors who all have something amazing to say. Your investment of only $12.95 per month is 100% GUARANTEED, and you may cancel at any time.

To order **MASTERS** CD-of-the-month program, or for information on any other MASTERS motivational tools, visit our Web site, e-mail, write, FAX, or call:

Order by phone:	(800) 459-4007 toll free
FAX:	(949) 497-7163
Order online:	www.MastersAudioClub.com
Order by mail:	**MASTERS**
	1278 Glenneyre, Suite 96
	Laguna Beach, CA
E-mail:	info@MastersAudioClub.com

MASTERS Audio Club ....$12.95 per month

Winn Claybaugh Seminars

It's one thing to entertain a group of people; it's another to inspire. Winn Claybaugh offers to companies, organizations, and businesses what he'd been looking for himself—someone to come in and properly motivate the staff.

Giants in their industries call on Winn to train and motivate their people. He's led seminars for Vidal Sassoon, the Irvine Company, Entertainment Tonight, Mattel, *For Rent* magazine, Structure/Limited Express, and many other businesses from hospitals to apartment communities.

Winn's classes provide concrete and comprehensive tools and ideas for making change, and they're a fun, "feel good" experience that improves productivity and helps organizations to increase their bottom line.

SHOT-IN-THE-ARM (2 hours): This lively event for up to 50 people stresses teamwork and personal motivation like nothing you've ever seen before.

UNBELIEVABLE CUSTOMER SERVICE: Learn to implement Winn's principles of Unbelievable Customer Service. Plan a long-term, profitable career; attract and retain the best type of client; establish *systems* to guarantee client happiness; and discover the secrets to creating high client retention.

DEVELOPING PIZZAZZ: Each participant leaves this hands-on motivational seminar with an individually designed vision for personal growth.

IT'S PAYDAY! Just because you give staff a paycheck, do they really feel compensated? Learn how to create "PAYDAY" every day; eliminate staff turnover; tap into your staff's incredible business creativity; and get your staff to "PLAY BIG" by practicing big!

Each seminar can be designed to meet the needs of your particular group. For more information, please contact:

Winn Claybaugh
1278 Glenneyre, Suite 96
Laguna Beach, CA
(800) 459-4007
FAX: (949) 497-7163
E-mail: info@BeNiceOrElse.com

PAUL MITCHELL THE SCHOOL

Whether your dream is to become a hairdresser, skincare therapist, or nail artist, **PAUL MITCHELL THE SCHOOL** has the program for you. As part of the internationally renowned Paul Mitchell hair care network, graduates of **PAUL MITCHELL THE SCHOOL** gain instant access to a host of successful salons and spas that will assist with recruiting, mentoring, support, and job placement.

The entire staff at **PAUL MITCHELL THE SCHOOL** is dedicated to helping graduates make their dreams come true and find the right home to begin their career—anywhere in the world! We're opening locations around the country, including schools in Rhode Island, Utah, California, and Florida.

To check out the courses offered at **PAUL MITCHELL THE SCHOOL,** find out how to enroll, or to learn about our team and more, please call, e-mail, write, or visit our Web site at:

PAUL MITCHELL THE SCHOOL
Attn: Admissions
1534 Adams Avenue
Costa Mesa, CA 92626
(877) 903-5375
info@PaulMitchellTheSchool.com
www.PaulMitchellTheSchool.com